Books by Janice Hardy

Foundations of Fiction Series
Planning Your Novel: Ideas and Structure
Planning Your Novel Workbook
Revising Your Novel: First Draft to Finished Draft

Skill Builders Series
Understanding Show, Don't Tell (And Really *Getting It)*

Novels
The Healing Wars Trilogy:
The Shifter
Blue Fire
Darkfall

PLANNING
Your Novel
WORKBOOK

Companion Book to Planning Your Novel: Ideas and Structure

Contains all the exercises and questions for
Planning Your Novel: Ideas and Structure
PLUS: Bonus questions on selected exercises

Janice Hardy

Fiction University's Foundations of Fiction

Contents

1   Welcome to the Planning Your Novel Workbook

3   Exercises for Workshop One: Finding Your Writer's Process
What Kind of Writer Are You?... 4
Assignment One: What Kind of Writer Are You? 5

6   Exercises for Workshop Two: Finding Ideas to Write About
Writing When You Don't Know What to Write About 7
Exercise: Narrow Down What Appeals to You.. 8
Where to Find Ideas.. 9
Exercise: Create Five Ideas for Possible Novels 10
Assignment Two: Choose Your Idea 11

12   Exercises for Workshop Three: Developing Your Idea
Brainstorming Your Idea 13
Exercise: Write Down Your Idea 14
Exercise: Revise Your Original Idea.. 15
Discovering Your Hook.. 16
Adding a New Twist to an Old Idea 17
Exercise: Craft Your Hook 18
Character-Driven or Plot-Driven? 19
Exercise: Determine What's Driving Your Novel—Character, Plot, or Both 20
Assignment Three: Flesh Out Your Idea... 21

22   Exercises for Workshop Four: Developing Your Characters, Point of View, Theme, and Setting
Discovering Your Characters 23
Choosing Your Main Characters... 24
Exercise: Determine the Main Characters in Your Novel 25
Identifying Your Protagonist 26
Exercise: Choose Your Protagonist 27
Identifying Your Antagonist.. 28
The Four Classic Conflict Types 28
Exercise: Determine the Type of Conflict in Your Novel 29
If the Antagonist is a Person.. 30

Exercise: Choose Your Person-vs.-Person Antagonist 32

If the Antagonist is Self 33

Exercise: Choose Your Person-vs.-Self Antagonist 34

If the Antagonist is Society 35

Exercise: Choose Your Person-vs.-Society Antagonist 36

If the Antagonist is Nature 37

Exercise: Choose Your Person-vs.-Nature Antagonist 38

Finding Your Character Arcs 39

Exercise: Determine Your Character Arcs 40

Choosing Your Point of View 41

Exercise: Choose a Point-of-View Style 42

Exercise: Determine Your Narrative Distance 43

Choosing Your Point-of-View Characters 44

Exercise: Choose Your Point-of-View Character 45

Writing From the Antagonist's Point of View 46

Exercise: Determine if You Want to Use the Antagonist's Point of View 47

Finding Your Theme 48

Exercise: Identify Your Theme 49

Choosing Your Setting 50

Exercise: Determine the Setting of Your Novel 52

Assignment Four: Flesh Out Your Characters, Theme, and Setting 53

54 Exercises for Workshop Five: Developing Your Plot

Welcome to Workshop Five: Developing Your Plot 54

Determining Your Goals 56

Exercise: Determine the Story and Plot Goals of Your Novel 57

Discovering Your Conflict 58

Finding Your Core Conflicts 59

Exercise: Determine Your Core Conflicts 60

Finding Your Stakes 61

Exercise: Determine Your Stakes 62

Assignment Five: Flesh Out Your Plot 62

64 Exercises for Workshop Six: Determining the Type of Novel You're Writing

Figuring Out Your Market 65

Exercise: Determine the Market for Your Novel 66

Figuring Out Your Genre 67

Exercise: Determine the Genre of Your Novel 68

Assignment Six: Finalize the Market and Genre of Your Novel 69

70 Exercises for Workshop Seven: Determining the Size and Scope of Your Novel

How Long Should Your Novel Be? 71

Exercise: Determine Your Target Word Count 72

Writing a Trilogy or Series 73

Exercise: Test Your Idea's Trilogy Potential 74

Should You Write the Whole Trilogy at Once? 75

Writing a Series 76

Exercise: Test Your Series Potential 77

Assignment Seven: Finalize the Size and Scope of Your Novel 78

79 Exercises for Workshop Eight: Turning Your Idea Into a Summary Line

Understanding the Summary Line 80
Exercise: Identify the Key Elements for Your Summary Line 81
Assignment Eight: Write Your Summary Line 83

84 Exercises for Workshop Nine: Turning Your Summary Line Into a Summary Blurb

Getting to the Heart of Your Story 85
Exercise: Determine the Goal of Your Novel 86
Getting to the Heart of Your Conflict 87
Exercise: Determine the Hooks of Your Novel. 88
Getting to the Heart of Your Setting 89
Exercise: Embed the Setting Into Your Novel 90
The Inciting Event 91
Exercise: Determine the Inciting Event of Your Novel. 92
Your Novel's Ending. 93
Exercise: Determine the Ending of Your Novel. 94
Exercise: Brainstorm Your Summary Blurb 95
Assignment Nine: Write Your Summary Blurb. 96

97 Exercises for Workshop Ten: Turning Your Summary Blurb Into a Working Synopsis

Defining Story Arcs 98
The Opening Scene 101
Exercise: Summarize Your Opening Scene. 103
The Inciting Event 104
Exercise: Summarize the Inciting Event. 105
The Act One Problem 106
Exercise: Summarize the Act One Problem 108
The Act Two Choice. 109
Exercise: Determine the Act Two Choice 111
The Midpoint Reversal 112
Exercise: Determine the Midpoint Reversal. 114
The Act Two Disaster 115
Exercise: Determine the Act Two Disaster 116
The Act Three Plan. 117
Exercise: Determine the Act Three Plan 118
The Climax 119
Exercise: Determine the Climax 120
The Wrap-Up 121
Exercise: Determine the Wrap-Up 122
Assignment Ten: Write Your Working Synopsis 123
Glossary 128

Welcome to the Planning Your Novel Workbook

When I first wrote *Planning Your Novel: Ideas and Structure*, I had no plans to do an accompanying workbook. But enough writers asked me for it and it sounded like fun, so I got to work.

This workbook is designed to work **with** *Planning Your Novel: Ideas and Structure (PYN)*. It's not intended to be used by itself, as there are no sessions or instructions here, only the questions and exercises from *PYN* with room to write down your answers. You'll also find bonus questions that aren't part of *PYN*—a little thank you for giving the workbook a try.

How to Use This Workbook

Some writers like to plan and develop their novels with pen and paper, and this workbook is all about brainstorming on paper and giving your muse a guide to follow. As you read through the *Planning Your Novel Workbook*, write down your answers and notes in the spaces provided in this workbook. Add extra pages of paper if you'd like, write in the margins, stick in Post-It Notes—whatever works for you. For those who like to create one workbook per novel idea, it probably won't be long before you're filling a workbook out without needing to reference the *PYN* sessions anymore.

Each workshop will list the page numbers for the corresponding workshop session in *Planning Your Novel: Ideas and Structure* (print version) for easy reference. If you're using the e-book version, please refer to the e-book's table of contents links to help you find the right sessions.

For those who haven't read *Planning Your Novel: Ideas and Structure*, I recommend starting there, and if you're the type who likes the organization of a workbook, use this book along with it.

Enjoy the workbook, have fun, and happy writing.

—Janice Hardy

Exercises for Workshop One: Finding Your Writer's Process

These exercises will help you determine the kind of writer you are and what (if any) changes you might want to make to your writing process. They'll explore different writing processes and show you how to examine your own process. (Pages 7-14 in *PYN*)

Re-Evaluating Your Writing Process

This is a great opportunity to re-evaluate your writing process. Sometimes it's useful to try new things to see if a small change can improve your process and make you a more productive writer.

As you go through these exercises, think about:

1. Doing a little more of something you already do.

You know what works for you, so why not give that aspect of your process a kick and see what happens? Look for elements you might benefit from if you did a little more of them.

2. Trying something you never thought would actually work for you.

Ask any writer how they write and you're bound to hear a few things that you either wouldn't try, or feel certain they would never work for you. But how do you know that for sure if you've never tried it? For all you know, that thing you're sure isn't for you is exactly what you need to double your word count per writing session.

3. Writing the next novel using a completely different process.

If you're frustrated or unhappy with your current process, try using something different for the next book. Dive in whole-heartedly and see what a new approach might gain you.

There's no right way to write. Find the process that works for you.

BRAINSTORMING QUESTIONS: What Kind of Writer Are You?
Discover your writing process. (Page 9 of *PYN*)

1. Which type of writer do you most identify with? (check all that apply)

    ❑ The Pantser   ❑ The Outliner   ❑ The Loose Outliner
    ❑ The Character Writer   ❑ The Plot Driver   ❑ The Scene Sewer

    How does this (or these) fit with your own writing style?

    _____

    _____

    _____

2. What style would you *want* to try? What about it appeals to you? Why?

    _____

    _____

    _____

3. What style *don't* you like? Why not?

    _____

    _____

    _____

4. Is your process working for you, or do you feel like it's holding you back?

    _____

    _____

    _____

5. If it's holding you back, why? What about the process do you find frustrating?

    _____

    _____

    _____

6. Can those frustrations be eliminated by trying or incorporating any of the other styles?

    _____

    _____

    _____

ASSIGNMENT ONE:
What Kind of Writer Are You?

>>Write down the type of writer you are and describe your writing process.

This might seem like a strange exercise, but I've found that I've learned more about writing from examining my own process and thinking honestly about *why* I do what I do, than from actually doing it.

Writing down your process lets you clarify exactly what it is you do when you write, and sometimes seeing it written down makes you realize that you're not what you thought you were. Maybe you actually *like* to outline a little, or prefer to develop a story organically based on a list of ideas, but rejected your natural process because you never saw yourself as "that kind of writer."

Writing down your process can also reveal areas that aren't working for you, and identify areas that could be improved to make writing easier overall.

For example:

▶ I like to know all about my characters before I start writing, plotting out how they're going to develop and what lessons they'll learn by the end of the book.

▶ I like a blank sheet of paper and a vague idea. Figuring out how the random details in my head all fit together makes me excited to write the book.

▶ I like planning out my scenes in detail, but don't care how they fit together until I'm almost done with the novel. I need to work out who the characters are as I write them and how the plot might work before I can see how the bigger picture looks.

_____

_____

_____

_____

_____

_____

_____

_____

_____

_____

_____

Exercises for Workshop Two: Finding Ideas to Write About

These exercises will help you find ways to come up with ideas and places to find inspiration. Feel free to mix and match any of the questions to better suit your process. (Pages 15-24 in *PYN*)

Working With Not-So-Original Ideas

There really *are* no new ideas out there. Every novel you pick up will have another book, TV show, or movie that did that idea. It's impossible to be unique in fiction these days. While that might sound like a huge downer, it's actually liberating. It gives us the freedom to write the ideas *we* like and feel excited about, and not worry so much if they've been done before because they probably have. What makes the idea fresh is how *we* treat it and how we bring that idea to the world.

When you're looking at a not-so-original idea, ask yourself:

What's different about my take on it? If there's nothing different in how you're doing it, then maybe you do have a done-to-death idea and should keep brainstorming. But if there are differences, and those differences take that idea to a new place, then it is a fresh idea.

What do I bring to the idea that hasn't been done before? Making a vampire the ultimate "bad boy" love interest was new when it was first done. Then others tried different paranormal creatures as hunky heroes and heroines. What about your idea *hasn't* been explored?

- Is there anything about this idea that always bothered you?
- Is there anything that seemed silly or too far-fetched you could riff off of?
- Is there an aspect you always wanted more information or history on?
- Is there an area that gets you especially excited?

Just because you have an idea that's been done by someone else doesn't mean you shouldn't write it. It might be harder to find a fresh twist to it, but it can be done.

What's different about *your* idea?

BRAINSTORMING QUESTIONS: Writing When You Don't Know What to Write About   Discover what stories and novels appeal to you. (Page 17 of *PYN*)

1. What kinds of novels are you drawn to? List your favorite books and what you love about them.

_____

_____

_____

2. What kinds of movies or TV shows are you drawn to? Make a list of your favorite movies and TV shows. Add what you love most about them.

_____

_____

_____

3. What similarities do you see? Is there a clear common genre or category?

_____

_____

_____

4. What recurring story or themes do you see? Do these elements spark any ideas?

_____

_____

_____

5. Is there a recurring type of character? Write down common traits in both the protagonist and the antagonist.

_____

_____

_____

6. Are there recurring plots? What are they?

_____

_____

_____

Bonus Question. What stories do you wish *you'd* written? Why?

_____

_____

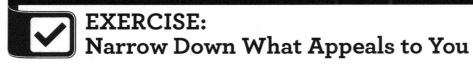

EXERCISE:
Narrow Down What Appeals to You

This is an exercise where making a list can aid you in determining what types of stories appeal to you. You might not know at first why a particular book resonates with you, but once you see a list of what you enjoy reading, a pattern may emerge.

Don't think too hard on these. The first answers will likely be the most revealing answers.

>>Write down:

1. The three genres or novel types that most interest you

_____

_____

_____

2. The three types of plots you most enjoy

_____

_____

_____

3. The three types of characters you're most drawn to

_____

_____

_____

4. The three themes that appear most often in the stories you enjoy

_____

_____

_____

5. The three settings you'd most like to write about

_____

_____

_____

Bonus Question. The three books you'd most like to emulate

_____

_____

_____

BRAINSTORMING QUESTIONS: Where to Find Ideas
Come up with some ideas. (Page 20 of *PYN*)

1. Pick three news articles or blog posts that intrigue you. What about them do you find compelling?

_____

_____

_____

2. What location have you always wanted to visit? What secrets might it be hiding?

_____

_____

_____

3. Pick your top ten images. What about them do you find captivating? Why?

_____

_____

_____

4. What are your favorite names? Why? What happens when you turn those names into names that would fit another genre, nationality, or ethnic group?

_____

_____

_____

5. What are your least favorite novels, TV shows, or movies? How would you write them differently?

_____

_____

_____

6. What random conversations or people caught your eye recently? Why were they memorable?

_____

_____

_____

Bonus Question. How would you rewrite your favorite novel or movie plot?

_____

_____

EXERCISE:
Create Five Ideas for Possible Novels

>>**Using the list from the first exercise, and the brainstorming questions from "Where to Find Ideas," list five combinations you might want to explore further.**

Now is the time to mix and match and put together the story types you enjoy with the topics that interest you. Use as many or as few as you'd like. If you're really stuck, try picking one item from each of the first exercise bullets and seeing where that leads you. Add in anything from the brainstorming questions that might fit that type of novel. If that doesn't spark an idea, try flipping it and picking one thing from each of the brainstorming questions.

For example:

▶ If you'd like to write a thriller, try picking a news article that sounds intriguing, then set it in the location that most appeals to you—such as a medical thriller about stem cell research set in Taiwan.

▶ If you love heist capers, pick your favorite art piece and figure out how your character would steal it—such as an art thief tries to steal the *Mona Lisa* from the Louvre.

▶ If you love stories about redemption, try choosing a news story about a truly despicable person and come up with a way for her to redeem herself—such as a woman who killed her children tries to make amends by saving a family in trouble.

For those stuck, pick:

■ One genre or novel type that most interests you (e.g., fantasy)

_____

■ One type of plot you most enjoy (e.g., heist)

_____

■ One type of character you're most drawn to (e.g., the dark hero)

_____

■ One theme that appears most often in the stories you enjoy (e.g., personal sacrifice)

_____

■ One setting you'd most like to write about (e.g., the Arctic)

_____

And put it all together:

For example:

▶ A fantasy heist plot, set in an arctic environment, with a dark hero who will have to make a personal sacrifice

_____

_____

_____

_____

ASSIGNMENT TWO:
Choose Your Idea

>>**Pick one of the ideas you came up with in Workshop Two to develop into a novel.**

These don't need to be full-fledged novel ideas, just things that pique your interest and make you want to explore them further, or a spark of inspiration that makes you think, "Gee, this would make a really great book."

If you're torn, pick the ideas that most interest you and decide later which is the strongest.

For example:

▶ A novel about teens with secrets, where one is bent on revenge
▶ A love story set during a zombie apocalypse
▶ A retelling of *Romeo and Juliet* with a twist

_____

_____

_____

Exercises for Workshop Three: Developing Your Idea

These exercises will help you develop the hook and general type of novel. You'll develop your idea, determine if your novel is character- or plot-driven, and find the hook that makes your novel unique. (Pages 25-51 in *PYN*)

What Every Story Needs to Do

I'm a big fan of the story. If I had to choose between a great story and great writing, I'd take story every time. Because without a great story, who cares about the writing? So, what does a great story have to do?

1. Hook the reader

2. Entertain them until the story is over

That's it. Seriously. It sounds so easy, but this is probably the number-one reason most well-written novels fail or never make it past the manuscript stage.

As you do these exercises, keep these two rules in mind. Hook readers by offering them something that makes them curious enough to keep reading. Make them care and want to spend more time with this character, see what develops in this world, or explore this premise some more.

- **Introduce an interesting character with a problem.**
- **Introduce a compelling situation.**
- **Introduce an intriguing character with a unique perspective.**

No matter how you hook your readers, entertaining your reader until the end of the story is the harder rule. There's no formula (though there is a reliable structure that works well); you just keep offering something readers find interesting and keep them wanting more.

Don't just write a good book. Tell a great story.

BRAINSTORMING QUESTIONS: Brainstorming Your Idea

Consider how the following question might apply to your idea. (Page 26 of *PYN*)

1. Who wants what and why?

_____

_____

_____

2. Who would be against these goals and why?

_____

_____

_____

3. Is there one major conflict or problem that needs solving?

_____

_____

_____

4. Who is the most likely person to be involved in this problem on a personal level?

_____

_____

_____

5. Where can huge failures occur?

_____

_____

_____

6. What situations would lend themselves well to the growth of a character?

_____

_____

_____

Bonus Question. What is it about this idea that makes you want to write it?

_____

_____

_____

EXERCISE:
Write Down Your Idea

If you've already done this in Assignment Two, you can skip this exercise.

>>Write down your idea.

Don't worry if it's vague or unformed at this stage, or if the idea is "bad." The goal is to get it on paper so you can study it and determine if it has what it needs to become a novel. It's so you can keep track of that original spark of inspiration and refer to it later when needed. It's not uncommon to lose track of where you want the novel to go or what inspired you about your novel in the first place, and having your original idea written down can remind you if the story goes off track later.

This will also give you some direction so later exercises can be more focused and more productive.

For example:

- ▶ Three teens with dark secrets meet at a diner in the middle of the night and change each other's lives
- ▶ A story set during a zombie apocalypse, where a guy was about to ask for a divorce when the world just fell apart, and now he wants to find his true love and not get eaten
- ▶ A *Romeo and Juliet*-type romance between old friends, set in a small town

If your idea is longer than these examples, that's okay. Write down as much or as little as you want. The first step in planning a novel is knowing what you want to write about.

_____

_____

_____

_____

EXERCISE:
Revise Your Original Idea

>>Go back to your idea and include any additional notes and thoughts.

How did your idea change? What do you know now that you didn't then?

Don't worry if you still have generalities in the idea. You might know that something brings your characters together, but not the specific details about it yet. It's okay at this stage to just know conceptually what you want to have happen. If you know specific details, that's great, too.

For example:

▶ Three teens with dark secrets meet at a diner in the middle of the night, each with a reason for being there that isn't what they claim.

▶ A love story set during a zombie apocalypse, where a guy wants a divorce but can't have it because the world just fell apart, and he needs his wife's survival skills to stay alive and help him find the woman he really wants to be with.

▶ Two childhood friends from feuding families reunite when the death of a favorite teacher causes them to return home.

_____

_____

_____

_____

_____

_____

_____

_____

BRAINSTORMING QUESTIONS: Discovering Your Hook
Explore what's compelling and different about your novel. (Page 36 of *PYN*)

1. List three critical things about your protagonist.

_____

_____

_____

2. List three critical elements of your conflict.

_____

_____

_____

3. List three critical things about your theme.

_____

_____

_____

4. List three critical things about your setting.

_____

_____

_____

5. List three critical things about your novel concept.

_____

_____

_____

Bonus Question. List three cool or unique things about this idea.

_____

_____

_____

Does anything on your lists jump out as a strong hook? What feels compelling or offers a new twist to an old idea? What best shows the strength of your novel?

_____

_____

BRAINSTORMING QUESTIONS: Adding a New Twist to an Old Idea
If your idea has already been done, explore ways to add a new twist to it. (Page 40 of *PYN*)

1. Is there a character type who's totally different from what's come before?

_____

_____

2. Can the setting make your idea different? Shift it into the future or the past?

_____

_____

3. Can you change the culture?

_____

_____

4. Can you play with the narrator's perspective?

_____

_____

5. Is there an aspect of this idea that hasn't been explored?

_____

_____

6. Could you add something from another genre to it?

_____

_____

7. Could you do it in a totally different genre than expected?

_____

_____

8. Are there any common tropes you could turn upside down?

_____

_____

9. Are there any rules you could play with? A "never do..." or an "always do..." you could ignore?

_____

_____

10. If you didn't do *anything* on the common tropes list, what might you come up with?

_____

_____

EXERCISE:
Craft Your Hook

>>Write down your novel's hook.

While you want to find the "ooooh" factor, this hook doesn't need to be agent-ready quality. Focus on what makes your idea fresh and compelling. You'll also have time to develop this further as you learn more about your novel and characters.

For example:

▶ What if your worst enemy knew your darkest secret?

▶ A soap opera love story set in the zombie apocalypse

▶ *Romeo and Juliet* meets the Hatfields and McCoys in a small, southern town

_____

_____

_____

BRAINSTORMING QUESTIONS: Character-Driven or Plot-Driven?

Explore if you have a character-driven or plot-driven novel. (Page 44 of *PYN*)

1. What internal forces are causing your characters to act?

_____

_____

_____

2. What external forces are causing your characters to act?

_____

_____

_____

3. Does resolving the external problem resolve the internal?

_____

_____

_____

4. Where does your idea fall on the character-driven vs. plot-driven scale?

_____

_____

_____

Bonus Question. Do you think up characters or plots first? Why?

_____

_____

_____

Bonus Question. How do you see the characters growing or changing? Is the arc clear?

_____

_____

_____

Bonus Question. How do you see the plot unfolding? Are the steps clear or uncertain?

_____

_____

_____

EXERCISE: Determine What's Driving Your Novel—Character, Plot, or Both

>>Describe how your novel is plot- or character-driven (or both).

Use any notes taken during the workshop to help you. Add in any new information that might have come to you. Also, don't worry if your novel changes as you work on it. A plot-driven novel could develop a strong character arc in later workshops and that's okay. Understanding what drives the novel now is just a guide to help you develop it.

For example:

▶ **Character driven:** The dark secrets are the internal forces causing the three teens to act. They each came to the diner of their own free will to do something about their secrets. Their personal reasons will drive the plot and force internal, emotional changes over the course of the novel. The book is more about who they are and what their secrets are than what they're doing.

▶ **Plot driven:** The zombie apocalypse is the external force that triggers the survival plot. It also makes the protagonist realize he wants to be with the woman he loves, not his wife. Survival and being with the woman he loves matter more than how the protagonist changes. The bulk of the plot will focus on these elements.

▶ **Both plot and character driven:** The death and funeral of the favorite teacher is the external force that causes the protagonists to return to their hometown. Their reasons for being there are the internal forces, as the teacher affected each of them in some profound way. Fulfilling a promise to the teacher causes them to interact and eventually fall in love. The book is about the internal journey to fall in love, but the external actions in fulfilling the promise will drive much of the plot.

_____

_____

_____

_____

_____

_____

_____

_____

_____

_____

_____

ASSIGNMENT THREE:
Flesh Out Your Idea

>>Summarize your idea, focusing on what makes the novel compelling and what aspect (plot or character) it will focus on.

This assignment is about clarifying all the brainstorming and note taking you've done so far. Try pinpointing the elements of your idea that most excite you, and the direction you feel the novel will take moving forward.

Feel free to add questions *you* find intriguing or want to explore with this novel. The things that excite you about a story are the same ones that will likely excite a reader. These questions can also guide you later when thinking about the themes or important story arcs.

For example:

▶ A contemporary novel about teens with secrets, where one is bent on revenge and the intended victim is someone with secrets worth keeping. Ideas of secrets and truth will be explored, and how keeping dangerous secrets might affect someone. What *would* happen if your enemy threatened to reveal or even revealed your darkest secret?

▶ A love story set during a zombie apocalypse with a meek husband and an overbearing wife. Ideas of gender roles and marriage will be explored, contrasted against the backdrop of the zombie apocalypse. How might a guy bossed around by his wife handle the end of the world?

▶ A mash-up of *Romeo and Juliet* meets the Hatfields and McCoys. Ideas of how much your family should influence and affect your life will be explored. How far are two lovers willing to go when their families don't want them to be together for long-forgotten (or even stupid) reasons?

_____

_____

_____

_____

_____

_____

_____

_____

_____

_____

_____

_____

_____

Exercises for Workshop Four: Developing Your Characters, Point of View, Theme, and Setting

These exercises will help you develop your characters, choose a point of view, find your novel's theme, and determine the novel's setting. (Pages 52-120 in *PYN*)

Bringing Your Novel to Life

Plot might be what gets your characters from scene to scene, but the heart of your novel lies in the characters, where they live, how they see the world, and the big-picture issues they struggle with. As you go through these exercises, think about how you can connect those various elements and strengthen your novel as a whole.

Compelling characters create reader connections. The more real the people in your story feel, the easier it will be for readers to relate to them.

Your **point of view** will show your story's world and help readers understand it. It will allow them a deeper view and appreciation of your characters.

Your **setting** provides the world your story will exist in, and the richer you make it, the more time readers will want to spend in it.

And your **theme** will tie all of it together, giving every aspect a deeper meaning that resonates with readers long after they've finished the book.

Stories are about interesting people, solving interesting problems, in interesting ways.

BRAINSTORMING QUESTIONS: Discovering Your Characters

When deciding who is going to be part of your novel, try thinking about the types of roles you might need. (Page 54 of *PYN*)

1. Who are the people that are going to provide information to the protagonist?

_____

_____

_____

2. Who are the people who are going to get in the protagonist's way?

_____

_____

_____

3. What types of people are commonly found in the world/situation/city/job/environment your novel is set in?

_____

_____

_____

4. Who has the power?

_____

_____

_____

5. Who are the victims?

_____

_____

_____

6. Who are the wild cards?

_____

_____

_____

Bonus Question. What characters are you excited to write about?

_____

_____

_____

BRAINSTORMING QUESTIONS: Choosing Your Main Characters
Consider characters for your novel. (Page 57 of *PYN*)

1. What kinds of characters might be in this novel?

_____

_____

_____

2. Who are the good guys?

_____

_____

_____

3. Who are the bad guys?

_____

_____

_____

4. What characters are already forming?

_____

_____

_____

5. What characters do you know have to be there?

_____

_____

_____

Bonus Question. Which characters will play the largest roles?

_____

_____

_____

Bonus Question. Which characters will face the most conflicts?

_____

_____

_____

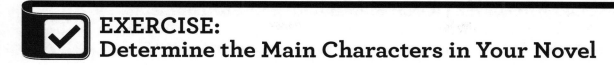

EXERCISE:
Determine the Main Characters in Your Novel

>>**List the main characters in your novel, and any information you know about them so far.**

These are the characters the novel is going to revolve around. They have the most to gain and lose, and they'll play a strong role in the novel's conflict. At this stage it isn't necessary to know protagonist and antagonist, but if you do know that, go ahead and write it down. It's also okay to write down any additional smaller characters that you think you might need or want.

For example:

► Lana (protagonist), Miguel, and Zachary (antagonist). A waitress at the diner. An unexpected diner who causes trouble.

► Bob (protagonist); his wife Sally (antagonist); Jane, the woman Bob is in love with.

► Adam and Hannah (protagonists). Adam's parents, Hannah's parents (the antagonists will come from these two families), the dead teacher, siblings or friends that are close to Adam and Hannah.

Sometimes you know you want a certain type of character, even if you don't know who they are yet. For example, you might know you need a best friend, but you haven't created that character yet. Or a love interest, or a rival. It's okay if the details of that character are still vague at this stage.

_____

_____

_____

_____

_____

_____

_____

BRAINSTORMING QUESTIONS: Identifying Your Protagonist

If you're not sure who your protagonist is, answer the questions with whoever is the best character for that role. If you do know who, how do these questions apply? (Page 59 of *PYN*)

1. Who has a problem that needs solving? What is that problem?

_____

_____

2. Who has the ability to act? How?

_____

_____

3. Who has reasons to act? What are they?

_____

_____

4. Who has something to lose? What is it?

_____

_____

5. Who has something to gain? What is it?

_____

_____

6. Who has the capacity to change? How so?

_____

_____

7. Who has a compelling quality? What is it?

_____

_____

8. Who has an interesting flaw? What is it?

_____

_____

9. Who has a secret? What is it?

_____

_____

10. Who has someone or something interesting blocking their way? Who or what is it?

_____

_____

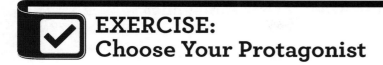

EXERCISE:
Choose Your Protagonist

>>Describe your protagonist in a few paragraphs or less.

Don't describe just the physical look (that's okay if you know it already), but the type of person he or she is and any history you might know at this stage. Try to get a sense of who this character is and how the novel might unfold with a protagonist like this.

For example:

▶ Lana is a cautious girl because she doesn't want anyone to know the truth about her. She deflects questions with humor, directing conversations back onto others. If anyone gets too pushy, she finds a way to start an argument and distract them, allowing her to storm out and escape. Because of this, she doesn't have a lot of friends.

▶ Bob is an average guy who's in an unhappy marriage with an aggressive woman. He never feels like he's good enough or man enough for her, which has created a major inferiority complex in him. The only bright spot in his life is Jane, a sweet, sensitive woman at his office. He's fallen in love with her, but is too scared to ask for a divorce or even tell Jane how he feels. His situation is made a lot worse when zombies attack, because now he clearly isn't strong enough to defend himself let alone take care of Jane. But he thinks maybe he can turn this disaster into a way to be the man he thinks is worthy of Jane.

▶ Adam is a headstrong entrepreneur who enjoys risks and pushing the edge. His favorite childhood teacher encouraged this, and he credits her for giving him the drive to escape his hometown and do something exciting and worthwhile with his life. Hannah is a shy introvert who wishes she were more daring, and she takes risks in quiet, unassuming ways. She also was influenced by this teacher, but never fully embraced the lessons to be the person she really wanted to be. The teacher's death comes at a time when both Adam and Hannah have just undergone traumatic events that make them question their lives.

_____

_____

_____

_____

_____

_____

_____

_____

_____

_____

BRAINSTORMING QUESTIONS: Identifying Your Antagonist
Here are things to consider when choosing and developing your antagonist. (Page 64 of *PYN*)

1. How did she/he/it get this way?

_____

_____

_____

2. Is there honor or nobility to the antagonist's actions?

_____

_____

_____

3. What tough choices have been made?

_____

_____

_____

4. What about the "evil plan" is actually *worth* pursuing?

_____

_____

_____

BRAINSTORMING QUESTIONS: The Four Classic Conflict Types
Here are things to consider when choosing and developing your antagonist. (Page 67 of *PYN*)

1. What type of conflict might prevent your protagonist from succeeding?

_____

_____

_____

2. What type of conflict might produce the best antagonist?

_____

_____

_____

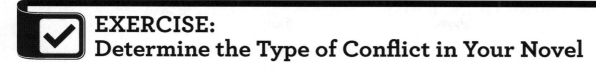

EXERCISE:
Determine the Type of Conflict in Your Novel

>>Write down the conflict type you feel would work best for your novel. Explain why.

It's okay if the details of that conflict are still unformed, but try to pinpoint the *type* of conflict if you can. Not only will this force you to consider the potential obstacles in your protagonist's way, it will make it easier later to determine what your core conflicts are, and how the antagonist fits into that conflict.

If you're not sure or think it could be a combination of conflicts, go ahead and write both down. You can pick a specific antagonist later in the workshop, and that choice should clarify which type of conflict you have. Sometimes it's not always clear, or you decide to change it as the novel develops.

For example:

▶ **Conflict Type:** Person vs. Person. The three teens will be against each other to resolve their issues. The other teens are the ones in the way of whatever each wants, and keeping them from being happy.

▶ **Conflict Type:** Person vs. Nature. The zombie apocalypse is a force the protagonist can't stop. He has to survive it to get what he wants. It could also be a Person vs. Person since he wants a divorce and his wife is keeping him from being with the woman he really loves.

▶ **Conflict Type:** Person vs. Person. Other people will be in the way of the two characters trying to keep their promise. Also, they could be in each other's way if they're trying not to fall for each other or get involved and make their families mad.

The conflict could change as you develop your novel, so don't worry if you have a few possibilities at this stage. If there are multiple types of conflict, you might decide to use all of them for different characters or plot arcs. What matters most is to think about the conflict and the areas where your characters are going to hit obstacles.

_____

_____

_____

_____

_____

_____

BRAINSTORMING QUESTIONS: If the Antagonist is a Person

Answer the following questions as they pertain to your novel. If you're not sure who your antagonist is yet, answer with whoever is the best character for that role. If you do know who your antagonist is, think about how these questions apply to him or her. (Page 71 of *PYN*)

1. What is this person trying to accomplish? Why?

    _____

    _____

    _____

2. What is this person's personal desire? Why?

    _____

    _____

    _____

3. How is this person motivated to act? Why?

    _____

    _____

    _____

4. What is this person trying to avoid? What happens if she doesn't?

    _____

    _____

    _____

    _____

5. What is this person trying to gain? What happens if she doesn't?

    _____

    _____

    _____

    _____

6. How might this person adapt?

    _____

    _____

    _____

7. How is this person compelling?

_____

_____

_____

8. What are this person's flaws?

_____

_____

_____

9. What are this person's strengths?

_____

_____

_____

10. What is this person hiding?

_____

_____

_____

11. How does this person stand in your protagonist's way?

_____

_____

_____

_____

_____

Bonus Question. What's redeemable about this person?

_____

_____

_____

Bonus Question. What will make readers like this person?

_____

_____

_____

EXERCISE:
Choose Your Person-vs.-Person Antagonist

>>Describe your antagonist.

Don't just describe the physical look (that's okay if you know it already), but the type of person he or she is and any history you might know at this stage. Try to get a sense of who this character is and how the novel might unfold with an antagonist like this.

For example:

▶ Zachary is the mastermind behind the plan, tricking the others into coming to the diner and pretending to be just as clueless as them about why they're there. He's cunning, manipulative, and consumed with revealing the secrets of the other two for his own nefarious purpose. This obsession is his weakness and causes him to push things farther than he should and risk revealing his own secrets.

▶ 1. The zombies are the villains, because they want to eat people. 2. On a more personal level, Sally is an antagonist because she's keeping Bob from Jane, the love of his life. Sally is tired of Bob's failure to live up to the potential she first saw in him when they were dating, and she thinks that if she pushes him hard he'll step up. When he doesn't, she gets angry and takes it out on him. The more he depends on her for survival, the less respect she has for him and the more she feels he can't possibly survive on his own. 3. A government guy, who came up with the zombification virus and is up to no good.

▶ The feuding families don't want Adam and Hannah to be together, because they've hated each other for generations. Adam and Hannah carry that prejudice, and this makes their feelings for each other very confusing for them. They resist for dumb, outdated reasons and a sense of family loyalty, even though being with each other is what will make them both happy.

_____

_____

_____

_____

_____

_____

_____

_____

_____

_____

_____

BRAINSTORMING QUESTIONS: If the Antagonist is Self

Here are some things to consider when choosing an antagonist for a Person-vs.-Self novel. (Page 75 of *PYN*)

1. Who or what in the novel represents what the protagonist is fighting?

_____

_____

_____

2. Who or what in the novel represents what the protagonist is struggling toward?

_____

_____

_____

3. What place represents what the protagonist is fighting?

_____

_____

_____

4. What item represents what she's fighting?

_____

_____

_____

Bonus Question. How is the protagonist hurting herself?

_____

_____

Bonus Question. What about the protagonist needs fixing?

_____

_____

_____

Bonus Question. Which character(s) is particularly bad for the protagonist?

_____

_____

_____

EXERCISE:
Choose Your Person-vs.-Self Antagonist

>>**Describe how your protagonist is also the antagonist.**

>>**Describe the person who represents the antagonist.**

Don't just describe the physical look (that's okay if you know it already), but the type of person he or she is and any history you might know at this stage. Try to get a sense of who this character is and how the novel might unfold with an antagonist like this.

BONUS TIP: Even if you have a Person-vs.-Person antagonist, it can be helpful to think about how your protagonist might be messing up her own life. Try doing this exercise to also find the flaw in your protagonist and how that hurts her in her quest to reach her goal.

For example:

▶ Lana is letting her secret control her and ruin her life, because she can't see how it's pushing everyone away and driving her toward destructive behavior. Miguel represents the antagonist for her personal struggle, because he's trying to reach her and knows she's in trouble, but she won't let him help her. Allowing Miguel to help her will let her shed the pain of her secret and escape the torment it's caused her for years.

▶ Bob is letting his insecurity rule his life and keep him from what he wants. If he stood up for himself, he'd be able to divorce Sally and be happy. He might even become the man Sally married again and work things out with her. The zombies represent the dangerous aspect of Bob's flaw because they're slaves to mindless actions that will never satisfy them. They also represent the overwhelming feeling of helplessness in the face of adversity, because Bob can't defend himself against them, same as he can't stand up to Sally. Bob needs to stand up and defeat the zombies, defend the women in his life, and take care of himself before he can see he does have value as a man and a husband.

_____

_____

_____

_____

_____

_____

_____

_____

_____

BRAINSTORMING QUESTIONS: If the Antagonist is Society

Here are some additional things to consider when picking a Person-vs.-Society antagonist. (Page 80 of *PYN*)

1. Who represents what the society stands for?

_____

_____

_____

2. Who is in the way of what the protagonist is trying to do?

_____

_____

_____

3. Why does the society believe in stopping the protagonist?

_____

_____

_____

4. Does the antagonist sympathize with the protagonist's argument?

_____

_____

_____

Bonus Question. What is noble about the society?

_____

_____

_____

Bonus Question. What part of the society does the protagonist agree with?

_____

_____

_____

Bonus Question. What is the biggest conflict about the society?

_____

_____

_____

EXERCISE:
Choose Your Person-vs.-Society Antagonist

>>**Describe the society and how it works as the antagonist.**

It's okay if you don't know every detail at this stage. Just try to get down the basic conflict that will help develop your antagonist.

For example:

▶ The government established a law in order to prevent a greater problem, but the people who are trying to uphold a "greater good" are sacrificing innocents to an unjust law. People have given up their rights to due process in order to punish those trying to tear apart their society. At first it worked, and allowed police to arrest criminals with far less evidence, but before long the "laws" became more and more strict and unfair. The slightest infraction can land someone in jail for decades. Society is the antagonist because the law is what caused the man's wife to be imprisoned, even though she didn't really do anything. He has to fight those who uphold the law to free her. He has to change society to get what he wants.

▶ A town rich in diamonds has made a deal with the inhabitants. They're cared for and protected as long as they send every child to the mines to work for four years. Children are eligible at age fourteen, and given a "starter kit" upon completion of their service—a place to live, a little money, and a job. The children have no say in where they go or what they'll do after. The society is the antagonist because no one wants to change things, and the law is about to send the protagonist into the mines. She doesn't want that and fights against the law to be free.

▶ A woman questions why she can't go to school like her brother in a world where women aren't allowed an education. They're given basic classes through elementary school, then sent to learn womanly trades to serve them in a marriage or household capacity. Any attempt to speak out is severely punished. Society is the antagonist because the cultural norm of not educating women has created an oppressed class who have no say over their lives. The protagonist fights this oppression by trying to change the tradition and be allowed to attend school.

_____

_____

_____

_____

_____

_____

_____

_____

BRAINSTORMING QUESTIONS: If the Antagonist is Nature

Here are things to consider when picking a Person-vs.-Nature antagonist. (Page 84 of *PYN*)

1. What's the purpose of nature in the novel?

   _____

   _____

   _____

2. What does nature represent?

   _____

   _____

   _____

3. How does nature challenge the protagonist over the course of the novel?

   _____

   _____

   _____

   _____

Bonus Question. What are three ways nature can cause trouble for the protagonist?

   _____

   _____

   _____

   _____

Bonus Question. What are three ways nature might help the protagonist?

   _____

   _____

   _____

   _____

Bonus Question. What about the nature antagonist appeals to you?

   _____

   _____

   _____

   _____

EXERCISE:
Choose Your Person-vs.-Nature Antagonist

>>Describe how nature is the antagonist.

It's okay if you don't know every detail at this stage. Just try to get down the basic conflict that will help develop your antagonist.

For example:

▶ The blizzard is the antagonist because the protagonist has to survive it in order to get home. It creates obstacles to everything the hero tries to do, and his only recourse is to find a way to ride out the storm.

▶ The forest is the antagonist because it stands between the kids and getting home. It doesn't care if they do or not, but all their obstacles come from dealing with the forest and what lives there.

▶ The storm is the antagonist because it's keeping the fishermen from getting back to port, and it might sink them and kill them all. They have to battle it to stay afloat and make it home.

_____

_____

_____

_____

_____

_____

_____

_____

BRAINSTORMING QUESTIONS: Finding Your Character Arcs
Things to think about when creating character arcs. (Page 87 of *PYN*)

1. Where do you want the character to end up?

_____

_____

_____

2. What does the character need to suffer through to achieve this change?

_____

_____

_____

3. Who or what brings about that change?

_____

_____

_____

4. How might the changes be for the worse?

_____

_____

_____

5. How might the character grow in the opposite direction of his or her goal?

_____

_____

_____

6. How does the change reflect the premise or theme?

_____

_____

_____

Bonus Question. How does the character arc affect the plot arc?

_____

_____

_____

EXERCISE:
Determine Your Character Arcs

>>Describe how your main characters might grow or change over the course of the novel.

Be as detailed or as vague as you need to at this stage. You might know the protagonist needs to "learn to accept her limits" but not specifically how she'll do that. The arc is about coming to terms with personal limits.

Feel free to create arcs for as many characters as you wish, and write as much or as little as you need to.

For example:

▶ Lana learns to trust others (through trusting Miguel) and realizes her past doesn't define her. A mistake can be just a mistake. She's able to redeem herself for letting someone get hurt by stopping Zachary from hurting others. Zachary doesn't learn this lesson, playing the dark side of Lana's arc, a look at what she could become if she doesn't change her ways. Miguel is caught in the middle, and he discovers his own inner strengths by standing up to the others.

▶ Bob starts out as a hopeless and helpless mess, but as he's forced to fight to survive, he gains confidence. His constant battles for life and death make him realize that life is indeed short and he could lose so much in an instant. He has to be strong and tell Jane he loves her, and make peace with Sally and their failed marriage. Overcoming the zombies is like cutting out the rot and decay in his own life and soul.

▶ Adam and Hannah are both wounded by events in their past caused by the family feud. Their teacher helped both of them break out of the destructive patterns of behavior and escape the town, but now that they're back, they're being sucked into it again. By accepting each other, they can help end the feud, but first they have to accept themselves and stand up to the families that caused the original traumas. As they deal with individual family members, they realize the truth behind the feud and find the solution to ending it. Ending it and making peace with their families heals the wounds and allows them to move on. Their relationship is the symbol of a new beginning for them and the families, healed and able to move forward again.

_____

_____

_____

_____

_____

_____

_____

_____

_____

BRAINSTORMING QUESTIONS: Choosing Your Point of View

Determine which point of view would work best for your novel. (Page 90 of *PYN*)

1. Which point-of-view style do you prefer?

   _____

   _____

   _____

2. How close do you want the reader to get to the characters?

   _____

   _____

   _____

3. What's common for the genre?

   _____

   _____

   _____

4. Is this a personal story or an epic tale?

   _____

   _____

   _____

5. What scope do *you* want to show? An epic tale, a personal struggle, or somewhere in between?

   _____

   _____

   _____

6. Who has the freedom to act?

   _____

   _____

   _____

7. Multiple or single point of view?

   _____

   _____

   _____

EXERCISE:
Choose a Point-of-View Style

>>Write down which point-of-view style appeals to you and why.

Sometimes a novel demands to be written in a style you don't normally write in, so don't worry if your favorite or natural style isn't right for a certain idea. You can decide if you want to try something new, or find a way to make the idea better fit the point-of-view style you want to write in.

For example:

- ▶ Third person omniscient, because it allows seeing inside the heads of all three teens and will enable the book to show things the characters might not know

- ▶ First person, because it's Bob's story and he doesn't know what's going on, so seeing things from his perspective will make it feel more personal and scary

- ▶ Third person limited, because it allows the reader to be inside the heads of the two major characters

_____

_____

_____

_____

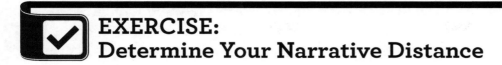

EXERCISE:
Determine Your Narrative Distance

>>Write down which narrative distance appeals to you and why.

Knowing how close or how far away you want the reader to feel can help you decide which point-of-view style would best suit your novel.

For example:

- ▶ Far narrative distance, because the observer feeling will add to the mystery and suspense of what's really going on

- ▶ Close narrative distance, because being inside Bob's head and having limited information will add to the personal nature and help raise the tension and stakes

- ▶ Close narrative distance, because being inside the heads of the romantic leads will let the reader see why these two belong together

_____

_____

_____

_____

BRAINSTORMING QUESTIONS: Choosing Your Point-of-View Characters
Answer the following questions with each of your potential point-of-view characters in mind. (Page 104 of *PYN*)

1. If you don't see that character's point of view, what is lost?

_____

_____

_____

2. Does every potential point-of-view character have her own plot or story goal?

_____

_____

_____

3. How do the points of view work together to tell a larger story?

_____

_____

_____

4. Which characters have the most to gain or lose?

_____

_____

_____

5. Is more than one of these points of view needed?

_____

_____

_____

6. If so, what do the multiple points of view allow you to accomplish?

_____

_____

_____

Bonus Question. What's unique about this point of view?

_____

_____

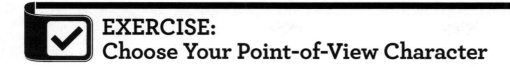

EXERCISE:
Choose Your Point-of-View Character

>>**Write down your point-of-view character(s) and explain why they make the best point of view for the novel.**

Don't forget to consider what the point-of-view character brings to the story. If the character is important enough to have part of the novel in her perspective, then she'll directly affect plot and not be there solely to convey information to readers.

For example:

▶ Lana, Miguel, and Zachary. The story is about these three and what secrets they're keeping, so seeing what's in their heads will help create mystery.

▶ Bob, because it's his story and seeing the plot unfold through his eyes will allow the reader to connect with him and want to see him win.

▶ Adam and Hannah, because they're the love interests and readers need to get to know them and see who they are from their perspectives in order to want to see them live happily ever after together.

_____

_____

_____

_____

_____

_____

_____

BRAINSTORMING QUESTIONS: Writing From the Antagonist's Point of View
Explore why you might show your novel from the antagonist's perspective. (Page 107 of *PYN*)

1. What does the antagonist bring to the plot that can't be seen otherwise?

   _____

   _____

   _____

2. Does the antagonist have a story arc or is she just there to tell the reader information?

   _____

   _____

   _____

3. Will the plot be spoiled if the reader sees what the antagonist is doing?

   _____

   _____

   _____

4. Can tensions be raised if readers see the antagonist in action?

   _____

   _____

   _____

5. How much of the book would appear in the antagonist's point of view?

   _____

   _____

   _____

6. Are you considering this point of view to make it easier or because it makes the book better?

   _____

   _____

   _____

Bonus Question. How does seeing the antagonist's point of view make her sympathetic?

   _____

   _____

   _____

EXERCISE: Determine if You Want to Use the Antagonist's Point of View

>>Decide if the antagonist's point of view is needed or not.

>>If yes, describe why the antagonist's point of view is needed and how it will benefit the novel.

For example:

▶ Yes. Knowing what's going on in Zachary's head will help create mystery because he'll know things the others don't, and they'll be making assumptions and decisions based on wrong information. Readers will see things are not what Lana and Miguel think, but not know the whole story because Zachary has things he won't admit even to himself.

▶ No, because seeing that Sally actually does care for Bob and is trying to do what she thinks is best for him will reveal that too early and make Bob's struggles less meaningful. Sally also doesn't have a different enough plot arc to sustain her own point of view and make it feel different from Bob's.

▶ No, because the antagonist role is played by multiple family members and none of them have their own storyline to warrant a point of view.

_____

_____

_____

_____

_____

_____

_____

_____

BRAINSTORMING QUESTIONS: Finding Your Theme
Explore possible themes for your novel. (Page 109 of *PYN*)

1. What larger concepts do you want to explore with your novel?

_____

_____

_____

_____

2. If you had to pick one cliché or adage to describe your novel, what would it be? How might you adapt that as your theme?

_____

_____

_____

_____

3. What are common problems in the novel? Do they point to a theme?

_____

_____

_____

_____

4. What are common character flaws or dreams?

_____

_____

_____

_____

Bonus Question. What recurring symbols or images are there?

_____

_____

_____

Bonus Question. What's the one word that sums up the novel's theme?

_____

_____

_____

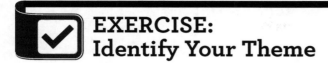

EXERCISE:
Identify Your Theme

>>State your theme.

Write down the theme of your novel. If there are any character themes, write those down as well. Be as specific or as vague as you need to at this stage. If you have only a general idea so far, that's okay. You can always refine it later.

For example:

▶ **Novel theme:** Secrets can ruin lives. **Story theme:** Things are never what they seem. **Character theme:** The truth can set you free.

▶ Courage through adversity, standing up for yourself to get what you want

▶ Love shall prevail

_____

_____

_____

_____

💡 BRAINSTORMING QUESTIONS: Choosing Your Setting

Here are some things to consider when choosing a setting. (Page 115 of *PYN*)

1. Where are *your* favorite places? List five locations you love.

   _____

   _____

   _____

   _____

   _____

2. What atmosphere do you want the novel to have? Write down the novel's dominant mood.

   _____

   _____

   _____

3. What settings are common to your genre? List five favorite settings common to your genre.

   _____

   _____

   _____

   _____

   _____

4. What location would enhance the novel's conflict and/or theme? List five locations that enhance your novel's conflict. Do the same for the theme. Are any of them the same location?

   _____

   _____

   _____

   _____

   _____

5. Do you want a real or fictional location? Write down which type of location you prefer.

   _____

   _____

   _____

   _____

6. Is it a small scale (a house) or large scale (a state) location? Write down the scale of your setting.

_____

_____

7. Do you want an urban or rural area? Write down which type of area you prefer.

_____

_____

8. Does the protagonist know this place? Write down how well the protagonist knows the setting.

_____

_____

_____

9. Do you want a setting you're familiar with or something you'd need to research? List five familiar settings you think might work for your novel. List five more that you've always wanted to visit.

_____

_____

_____

_____

_____

Bonus Question. How many different settings do you anticipate having?

_____

_____

_____

Bonus Question. What do these settings bring to the story? How do they affect it?

_____

_____

_____

Bonus Question. Can any of these settings be the opposite of what you imagined? How might that affect the story?

_____

_____

_____

EXERCISE:
Determine the Setting of Your Novel

>>Describe your setting.

If you have more than one, describe all the important locations you might need. Don't worry if you're not sure, as more locations will no doubt occur as the novel unfolds. Focus on the general sense of the place or world as well. As a fun extra, try to explain why you chose this setting and what you feel it can add to the novel.

For example:

▶ Modern day, a rundown roadside diner just off a highway. It's dark, spooky, and a little foreboding to set the tone of the darkness of secrets and the danger ahead for the characters. School, in the areas where outcasts and the unpopular kids hang out. The scene of the original accident. Settings will all be "secretive" in some way to reinforce the theme of secrets. As the secrets slowly come out and become less important, the locations will become more and more public (the truth revealed). **Why I chose these settings:** These are all places where people hide things or hide the truth, which helps reinforce the theme of secrets.

▶ Cleveland, Ohio, not far from the Rock & Roll Hall of Fame, a favorite spot for Bob, who goes there to dream and escape his life. Locations change as the characters head south to a rural town rumored to be well-fortified against the zombies. The government lab where the cure can be found. An abandoned mall with zombies that look like mannequins at first and surprise them. Settings start out normal, then turn disastrous as the zombies take over and hope fades. But as Bob gains confidence, he starts seeing things in more hopeful and defensible ways. **Why I chose these settings:** These are places that show Bob's desire to be more than he is, and places where he's less than he wants to be (like home and on the road where he fails and is saved by his wife). They're also places to explore the horror factor and create cool situations with the zombies.

_____

_____

_____

_____

_____

_____

_____

_____

_____

_____

_____

ASSIGNMENT FOUR:
Flesh Out Your Characters, Theme, and Setting

>>**Summarize the characters in your novel, focusing on their character arcs and how they grow over the course of the novel. Also summarize how theme affects their character arcs, and how the setting influences how they feel about the world they live in.**

This assignment is designed to get you thinking about the connections among your characters, theme, and setting. You've developed them individually, but summarizing them as they relate to each other helps to establish and clarify how they work together. Some summaries might include the conflicts and plot aspects of the novel if they directly affect these elements, while others might focus solely on the character arc and emotional growth side.

Feel free to do this exercise with as many or as few characters as you'd like. You might find just doing the protagonist is enough, or you might want to do each major character. If you're not sure, consider which characters will have character arcs and use those, or use the character with the most story-driving arc. You can even combine characters if their arcs are closely linked to the novel.

Try this if you're still stuck on what to write:

1. List three critical details about the character—one that shows who she is, one that shows how she illustrates the theme, and one that shows how she illustrates the setting.

2. List the kind of person the character is at the start of the novel and at the end of the novel. Add a general description of how she gets from one to the other.

3. Create one to three sentences that contain all three traits and one to three sentences that summarize that journey, and then craft one connected paragraph that covers everything. Flesh out this paragraph with any additional details you'd like to add.

_____

_____

_____

_____

_____

_____

_____

_____

_____

_____

Exercises for Workshop Five: Developing Your Plot

These exercises will help you identify and develop the goals, conflicts, and stakes of your story so you can create a plot from them. (Pages 123-148 in *PYN*)

As you're developing your plot, don't forget to:

Be Flexible When Plotting Your Novel

Flexibility is something I think every writer can benefit from, no matter what kind of writer you are, be it an outliner or a pantser. Writing is an organic process, and when we allow ourselves to let that process happen, we can tap into our subconscious and piece together ideas we've never consciously thought about before. I believe inspiration and those exciting "Aha!" moments come from letting ideas churn in the backgrounds of our brains.

But having stories suddenly head off in new directions *can* be scary. You can feel like you don't have control over your story, that you don't know where you're going, even that you aren't a "real" writer because you're not following some perfect format or expectation. Getting scared is a good way to block yourself from writing at all—and who wants that?

Don't stress over it.

Take a deep breath and look at what's happening on the page. Even when your characters get out of control, you still *are* in control of them. The trick is knowing when to let them run and when to buckle down and break out the whip. For that, trust your instincts and give yourself the freedom to explore a little if it feels right.

Your gut is a pretty good compass. If it feels wrong, chances are it is, but if it feels right, then trust yourself and go with it. Be flexible and let your story reach for the heights you may not have yet realized it has.

Plot is how you illustrate your story to the reader.

💡 BRAINSTORMING QUESTIONS: Determining Your Goals
Explore possible character goals. (Page 131 of *PYN*)

1. What does your protagonist want?

_____

_____

_____

_____

2. What is your protagonist willing to do to get what she wants?

_____

_____

_____

_____

3. What are some possible goals (and steps) the protagonist might take to get what she wants?

_____

_____

_____

_____

_____

Bonus Question. What plot arcs do you see developing based on these goals?

_____

_____

_____

Bonus Question. What goals might conflict?

_____

_____

_____

Bonus Question. What goals might overlap in interesting ways?

_____

_____

_____

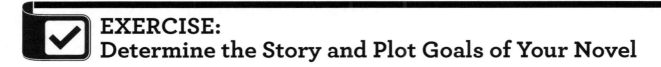

EXERCISE:
Determine the Story and Plot Goals of Your Novel

>>What are the story and plot goals of your protagonist and antagonist?

For example:

▶ **Protagonist: Story goal:** Lana wants to redeem herself for a past mistake that put her older brother in a wheelchair. Everyone thinks it was an accident, but she knows she caused it and it's all her fault, even if he doesn't remember. She wants to make it up to her brother, but has no idea how. **Plot goal:** To keep her secret when she's summoned to a diner in the middle of the night by someone threatening to expose her secret and ruin her.

Antagonist: Story goal: Zachary blames Lana and Miguel for something that happened to him and wants to destroy their lives as he thinks they destroyed his. **Plot goal:** To force Lana and Miguel to publicly confess what they did, which will exonerate him for a past deed he was wrongly accused of.

▶ **Protagonist: Story goal:** Bob wants to find happiness with Jane and escape his difficult marriage, regaining his freedom and his manhood. **Plot goal:** To survive the zombie apocalypse and divorce (or get rid of) his wife.

Antagonist: Story goal: Sally is trying to keep Bob and herself alive, hoping the zombie threat will force Bob to step up and not be a wuss all the time. **Plot goal:** To survive, and intentionally put Bob in dangerous situations to trigger his own survival instincts.

_____

_____

_____

_____

_____

_____

_____

_____

_____

_____

_____

_____

_____

BRAINSTORMING QUESTIONS: Discovering Your Conflict
Explore possible conflicts. (Page 135 of *PYN*)

1. What are some possible conflicts in your idea?

_____

_____

_____

_____

2. What characters might be in conflict with each other?

_____

_____

_____

_____

_____

3. What larger conflicts might occur in your world or setting?

_____

_____

_____

_____

Bonus Question. What are some possible internal conflicts?

_____

_____

_____

Bonus Question. What external conflicts might the protagonist encounter?

_____

_____

_____

Bonus Question. What situations will be the most difficult to resolve?

_____

_____

_____

BRAINSTORMING QUESTIONS: Finding Your Core Conflicts
Explore the major conflicts driving your characters and your novel. (Page 139 of *PYN*)

1. What are the external conflicts in the book? List five possible conflicts.

_____

_____

_____

_____

_____

2. How might these conflicts keep the protagonist from getting what she wants? List how and why.

_____

_____

_____

3. What are the internal conflicts in the book? List five possible ways your characters can be conflicted.

_____

_____

_____

_____

_____

4. How might the protagonist's personal beliefs hinder her in achieving her goal? List five possible ways her personal goals might conflict with her plot goals.

_____

_____

_____

_____

_____

5. What are the most critical conflicts, both externally and internally? List them and state why.

_____

_____

_____

_____

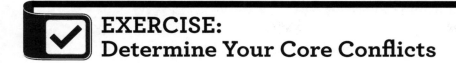

EXERCISE:
Determine Your Core Conflicts

>>Summarize your external and internal core conflicts.

It's okay if some things are still uncertain, especially if you like to discover your novel as you write it, but try to pinpoint your protagonist's goal and how it will drive your novel.

For example:

- ▶ **External Core Conflict:** Three teens are trying to figure out why they're all at the diner and who summoned them there. **Internal Core Conflict:** Trying to keep their secrets a secret.

- ▶ **External Core Conflict:** Bob is trying to survive the zombie apocalypse and win the woman he loves. **Internal Core Conflict:** Bob can't survive unless he stays with his wife, and he's struggling to feel worthy of surviving and being with Jane.

- ▶ **External Core Conflict:** Feuding families are trying hard to keep Adam and Hannah apart. **Internal Core Conflict:** Wanting to be together even though it would cause trouble with their families.

_____

_____

_____

_____

_____

_____

_____

BRAINSTORMING QUESTIONS: Finding Your Stakes

Explore possible stakes and determine if they're high enough, or personal enough to your protagonist to carry a novel. (Page 143 of *PYN*)

1. If the protagonist walked away, what would change?

_____

_____

_____

_____

2. If you put the second-most important character in the protagonist's slot, what would change?

_____

_____

_____

_____

3. What does the protagonist lose if she walks away from this problem?

_____

_____

_____

_____

4. What sacrifice does the protagonist have to make for everything to turn out the way she wants?

_____

_____

_____

_____

Bonus Question. Why should readers care about the protagonist failing?

_____

_____

_____

Bonus Question. What about the stakes is relatable to readers?

_____

_____

_____

EXERCISE: Determine Your Stakes

>>Describe your stakes.

What does the protagonist have to gain, what does she have to lose, and what are the consequences if she fails at her task?

For example:

▶ Lana's reputation and relationship with her family will be ruined if they find out the role she played in her brother's accident. The few friends she has left will shun her and she'll be an outcast at school. She fears she might even wind up in jail. But if she comes clean and redeems herself, she can shed the guilt that's making her sick and ruining her life anyway. She even has a chance of stopping Zachary, who played a role in the accident himself, though she's not aware of that. Uncovering his secrets will allow her to finally let go of hers.

▶ Bob's life and happiness. Zombies could eat him at any time. His wife could leave him behind to fend for himself, or he could lose Jane to zombies. She might reject him if she doesn't feel the same way. He might learn that he really is as pathetic as he fears and ought to be left behind as zombie food. But if he stands up and tries to be the man he wants to be, he'll find the strength to face the zombies and be able to tell Jane he loves her, and Sally he doesn't. He'll learn how to fend for himself on both a physical and emotional level.

▶ Adam could wind up alone and throwing himself into a job that's slowly eating his soul. He'll resent his family and cut off all ties with them. Hannah could listen to her family and give up her dream of adventure and love, returning to her hometown and living the life her family always pushed on her. But if they both listen to their hearts and stand up to their families, they can be together and fill the void each has in their lives. They'll find happiness and give each other the strength and support they need to overcome their weaknesses and be happy.

_____

_____

_____

_____

_____

_____

_____

_____

_____

ASSIGNMENT FIVE:
Flesh Out Your Plot

>>**Summarize the main goals, conflicts, and stakes of your novel and how they might create your plot.**

If you're really stuck on what to write try this:

1. List possible goals in your beginning, middle, and ending. Use story goals, personal goals, or both.

2. List possible conflicts in your beginning, middle, and ending. Use external conflicts, internal conflicts, or both.

3. List possible stakes in your beginning, middle, and ending. Use the personal stakes, story stakes, or both.

4. Combine everything and summarize where the plot might come from. Add in any details that help flesh out the goals, conflicts, and stakes listed.

For example:

▶ **Goals: Beginning**—to pretend everything is okay, to find out who summoned her to the diner. **Middle**—to keep her secret, to find out who is threatening to expose it. **Ending**—to find out what really happened to her brother, to stop Zachary and save Miguel.

Conflicts: Beginning—guilt makes her want to confess, but fear of reprisal keeps her quiet. **Middle**—fear of getting caught makes her want to run, but fear of exposure makes her want to stay and figure out who's behind this. **Ending**—she wants to expose the truth and Zachary, but he wants to ruin her through lies.

Stakes: Beginning—her family will disown her if they find out she caused her brother's accident. She'll be humiliated in front of everyone she knows. She might even wind up in jail. **Middle**—she'll never find out the truth about her brother and won't be able to redeem herself. **Ending**—she'll be blamed for the terrible things Zachary has planned, won't be able to find peace, and will lose her life and maybe even Miguel's life.

_____

_____

_____

_____

_____

_____

_____

_____

_____

_____

_____

_____

_____

_____

_____

_____

_____

_____

_____

_____

_____

_____

_____

_____

_____

_____

_____

_____

_____

_____

_____

_____

_____

Exercises for Workshop Six: Determining the Type of Novel You're Writing

These exercises will help you determine your novel's market and genre (if applicable). If you're not at the submission or publishing stage yet, don't worry about these aspects. Write for fun and enjoy the process. (Pages 152-167 in *PYN*)

Should You Know Your Genre First?

If you're writing with the intent to publish, knowing where your novel fits is helpful. There are elements to any genre that readers expect, and if you don't give them that, they'll be disappointed. Disappointed readers are very bad for a writer's career.

While you certainly don't have to know your genre and market before you start writing, it does make things considerably easier. The novel's category gives you a lot of information on how to write that novel. You'll know general word count range, what else has been published in that genre that's similar, what's popular, what's been done to death.

If you're unsure, the core conflict of a story almost always defines what that type of story is. As stories can be universal, look for the details of the story to help you there. Strong fantasy elements? Science fiction elements? Horror? Western? Thriller elements? The setting and details surrounding the problem can also help determine the genre, as does the path the protagonist takes to solve the problem.

If you think, "Well, I'm just writing a story," that's fine. You're probably writing general fiction. Not every book is genre (probably only about half, actually). If the story develops into a genre, great, if not, that's okay too. Stories change. They even turn into things that cross over boundaries and defy categorization.

Do as many of these exercises as you feel you need to do to understand your novel and where it fits into the market.

Genre can help shape a story to fit a reader's expectation.

BRAINSTORMING QUESTIONS: Figuring Out Your Market

Answer these questions to identify the market you want to write for. (Page 154 of *PYN*)

1. What are the ages of your main characters?

_____

_____

_____

2. What type of problem is the core conflict?

_____

_____

_____

3. What age group do you feel this novel would appeal to?

_____

_____

_____

4. In what section of the bookstore do you see this novel?

_____

_____

_____

Bonus Question. Who would you recommend this novel to?

_____

_____

_____

Bonus Question. What events might you attend to promote this novel? Who also attends those?

_____

_____

_____

Bonus Question. What other books are most like yours? What market are they?

_____

_____

_____

EXERCISE:
Determine the Market for Your Novel

>>Write down the market you feel your novel will most appeal to.

Try to pick the market that contains the majority of potential readers. While young adult novels are often read by adults, the market is still young adult, as that's how it would be promoted and that's who the target audience is.

For example:

▶ Young Adult: Three teen protagonists dealing with teen issues they will resolve without the aid of adults. (Three teens summoned to a diner in the middle of the night)

▶ Adult: Adult protagonist dealing with an adult problem he will resolve using adult thinking. (Bob, facing the zombie apocalypse while navigating a love triangle)

▶ Adult: Adult protagonists dealing with adult problems in adult ways. (Hannah and Adam falling in love and trying to bring peace to their feuding families)

_____

_____

_____

_____

_____

BRAINSTORMING QUESTIONS: Figuring Out Your Genre

Answer these questions to further pinpoint the type of novel you want to write. (Page 160 of *PYN*)

1. Where do you see this book on the shelves?

_____

_____

_____

2. What is the one defining characteristic of the novel?

_____

_____

3. What is the core conflict of the novel?

_____

_____

_____

4. What other books are similar to it?

_____

_____

5. What genres are *those* books categorized as?

_____

_____

6. What do *you* feel you're writing?

_____

_____

7. What are the key elements you use to describe the novel to people?

_____

_____

_____

8. What genre are *those* elements?

_____

_____

EXERCISE:
Determine the Genre of Your Novel

>>Write down the genre you feel best suits your novel. If it fits a subgenre, write that down as well.

If your novel is hard to classify, look for the strongest genre element. If there is no genre, remember that "fiction" is applicable.

For example:

- ▶ Mystery or suspense
- ▶ Science fiction with romantic elements
- ▶ Romance

_____

_____

_____

_____

ASSIGNMENT SIX:
Finalize the Market and Genre of Your Novel

>>Using all the notes you made in **Workshop Six**, choose which market your novel is targeting, and why this is the best market for it.

>>Choose which genre best suits it and state why.

>>Pick a subgenre if applicable, and state how this fits your novel.

For example:

▶ Young adult suspense, because the protagonist and main characters are teens dealing with teen issues. The goal of the book is to solve the puzzle and the mystery puts the characters' lives in danger. (Three teens summoned to a diner in the middle of the night)

▶ Adult science fiction with romantic elements, because the plot focuses on the zombie attacks, but the character arcs focus on the romance between Bob and Jane. The characters and problems are from an adult worldview. (Bob, facing the zombie apocalypse while navigating a love triangle)

▶ Adult romance, because the focus is on the relationship between two adults, Adam and Hannah, with the plot goal of overcoming their family issues. The end goal is for them to get together and live happily ever after. (Hannah and Adam falling in love and trying to bring peace between their feuding families)

_____

_____

_____

_____

_____

_____

_____

_____

_____

_____

_____

_____

_____

Exercises for Workshop Seven: Determining the Size and Scope of Your Novel

These exercises will help you determine the size and scope of your novel. They're especially useful for those trying to decide if they have a single novel, or a trilogy or series. (Pages 168-191 in *PYN*)

Sometimes we don't know the full scope of our novels until we write them, but plenty of writers envision a novel as a series before they write the first word. Knowing if it's a stand-alone novel or a series helps to plan the best way to handle that novel.

Just like with market and genre, it's not necessary to know the scope of your novel before you write it, but it can be a useful tool. It can help gauge where the major turning points are or when certain events need to happen.

If you're writing for fun or don't want to worry about word counts yet, do as many (or as little) of these as you'd like.

The right word count is the one that keeps the story moving.

BRAINSTORMING QUESTIONS: How Long Should Your Novel Be?
Pick five novels that best fit your chosen market and genre. Try not to choose mega-bestsellers, as these novels don't always fit the norm and are often outside the average. (Page 169 of *PYN*)

1. What is the word count for each novel?

To determine this, either look it up online (word count is sometimes part of the product details) or estimate it by taking the average of ten lines of text, then counting how many lines per page, and determining a per-page number. Then multiply that number by the page count. You can do this with a physical book or count in the "look inside" feature online.

For example:

- Pick the first full page of text in the novel
- Count the number of words in the first 10 lines (say it's 83 words)
- Divide that number by the number of lines (10) to get the average number of words (8 words per line)
- Now count the number of lines on the page (say it's 28 lines)
- Multiply the number of lines per page by the average number of words per line to get the average number of words per page (28 x 8 = 224 words per page)
- Multiply the average number of words per page by the number of pages to get the approximate word count (224 x 387 = 86,668 words in the novel)

_____

_____

_____

2. What is the word count range for all five novels?

_____

_____

3. Which novels are your favorites?

_____

_____

_____

4. What are the word counts for those novels?

_____

_____

5. What size feels like a good target word count for your novel?

_____

EXERCISE:
Determine Your Target Word Count

>>Write down the target word count for your novel.

This is a rough estimate, not something set in stone. The goal is to find a target size that will help you determine where classic story structure elements fall when you outline and/or write your novel. It will also give you an idea if your novel fits with your chosen market and genre or if it's outside the average.

For example:

▶ 60,000 words (a common word count range for a YA novel)

▶ 100,000 words (a common word count range for an adult science fiction novel)

▶ 80,000 words (a common word count range for an adult romance)

_____

_____

_____

BRAINSTORMING QUESTIONS: Writing a Trilogy or Series

Try breaking your trilogy idea into the three major turning points, and do a rough outline or quick summary of how it might unfold. (Page 173 of *PYN*)

1. What is the moment/event where the protagonist first realizes there's a larger trilogy problem? This is likely connected to the resolution and core conflict goal of Book One.

   _____

   _____

   _____

   _____

2. What is the moment/event where the protagonist first realizes she's completely in over her head and has only made things worse? This is likely connected to your Book Two core conflict and goal.

   _____

   _____

   _____

   _____

3. What is the moment/event where your protagonist realizes the only way to win is to resolve the trilogy goal? This is likely the core conflict and goal of Book Three.

   _____

   _____

   _____

   _____

4. How might you escalate the stakes at each of these stages? This is likely connected to your character arc in some way, as your protagonist has to make a sacrifice or face tougher choices.

   _____

   _____

   _____

   _____

5. What secrets might be revealed over the course of the trilogy? This is a good way to tie in your conflict arcs with your character arcs.

   _____

   _____

   _____

EXERCISE:
Test Your Idea's Trilogy Potential

Not every idea will be right for a trilogy, so if you're thinking about writing one, test it to see if it has what it needs to span three novels.

- Does each novel have a core conflict that can be resolved?

_____

_____

_____

- Does each novel have something personal at stake for the protagonist?

_____

_____

_____

- Do the stakes escalate in each book?

_____

_____

_____

- Does each novel trigger the next book?

_____

_____

_____

- Does the final book resolve a problem that has been building for three books and connects the previous core conflicts?

_____

_____

_____

If you answered yes to these questions, then you likely have a workable trilogy idea. If you answered no to one or two of them, you might want to develop your idea more before you start writing. If you answered no to three or more, you probably don't have a big enough idea for a trilogy yet.

Bonus Question. Are you padding your idea to *make* it into a trilogy? (Be honest.)

_____

_____

_____

BRAINSTORMING QUESTIONS: Should You Write the Whole Trilogy at Once?

Answer the following questions to determine whether or not to write the entire trilogy first. (Page 181 of *PYN*)

1. Can the first book stand alone even if you never write the others?

_____

_____

_____

2. Do you need to see how it ends before you'll feel confident submitting or publishing it?

_____

_____

_____

3. Do you know where the story is going or are you still figuring out the major parts?

_____

_____

_____

4. Do you have other novels you'd rather write or feel might be more marketable?

_____

_____

_____

5. Which way do *you* want to go?

_____

_____

_____

6. Will the trilogy be better if you write the whole thing at once? Worse?

_____

_____

_____

7. Do you want agent/editor/reviewer feedback before you write the rest?

_____

_____

💡 BRAINSTORMING QUESTIONS: Writing a Series
Answer the following questions about your potential series. (Page 183 of *PYN*)

1. Is your concept big enough to maintain multiple books? List five reasons why this series concept might hook readers.

_____

_____

_____

2. Is there enough conflict in the idea to sustain multiple books? List five potential problems that could be the core conflict for future books.

_____

_____

_____

3. Do you want your protagonist to change over the course of the series or stay the same? If she changes, describe a possible character arc that will take multiple books to resolve.

_____

_____

_____

4. In what time frame does the series take place? Describe the length of time you envision, and if it's open-ended or finite.

_____

_____

_____

5. Is your world or setting large enough to maintain interest over a series? Describe your setting or world and list five possible ways each might influence a book idea.

_____

_____

_____

6. Why would a reader return to this series after the first book? List five reasons why readers might invest time in this series.

_____

_____

_____

EXERCISE:
Test Your Series Potential

>>Develop five book ideas for your series and craft a one-line summary for each.

Sometimes an idea feels like it has the legs to become a series, but when you sit down to plot it out, you discover you can think up only a few ideas before it becomes the same plot with different details. Test your idea and see if it has enough depth to become a series.

>>If your protagonist changes, create a character arc and show the growth over those five books. Write down where you want your protagonist to end up by the end of the series.

You don't have to be detailed at this stage if you're still unsure. Knowing that your emotionally detached protagonist will eventually form solid commitments and relationships by the last book can be enough to get you started.

_____

_____

_____

_____

_____

_____

_____

_____

_____

_____

_____

_____

_____

_____

_____

_____

_____

_____

_____

_____

_____

_____

ASSIGNMENT SEVEN:
Finalize the Size and Scope of Your Novel

>>**Using all the notes you made in Workshop Seven, summarize:**

- Which market your novel is aimed at

_____

_____

_____

- Which genre best suits it

_____

_____

_____

- The subgenre if applicable

_____

_____

_____

- If it's a series and, if so, what kind

_____

_____

_____

If you've decided on more than one idea, answer for all. If this is a trilogy or a series, describe the overall series concept.

_____

_____

_____

_____

_____

_____

_____

_____

Exercises for Workshop Eight: Turning Your Idea Into a Summary Line

These exercises will help you take an idea and develop it into a one-sentence summary line you can build a novel from. Don't worry if your line is rough—it's just for you at this stage of the novel. (Pages 192-200 in *PYN*)

Capturing your entire novel in one sentence is one of the harder things to do, but a valuable tool in both writing and selling that novel down the road. You'll be telling people what your novel is about for a long time, and you'll want that one-sentence line to (eventually) roll off your tongue and make them say, "Ooh, I want to read that."

The summary line is where you'll start developing that awesome response to, "What's your book about?"

Focus on the heart of the novel, and what made you want to write it in the first place. This will not only guide you, but remind you why you love this novel when the writing gets tough.

The more clearly you can identify your conflicts, goals, stakes, and motivations, the easier the novel will be to write. You'll clearly know what has to happen to accomplish those goals, and what happens if they're not met.

You'll likely have to sift through a lot of your favorite things about the novel, so don't be afraid to mix and match what you like best. You never know where the right summary will come from. The things that stand out most strongly in your mind are most likely what will best serve the story and help you write it.

As you do these exercises, think about the things that will best help you write this novel.

The heart of the novel can be summarized in one sentence.

BRAINSTORMING QUESTIONS: Understanding the Summary Line
Think about the things that might go into your summary line. (Page 193 of *PYN*)

1. Identify who your protagonist is and what's unique about him or her. Try listing three or four things you might use. Pick the most critical details or traits readers would need to know about this person (or people if you have an ensemble cast).

   _____

   _____

   _____

   _____

   _____

2. Identify the most important elements of your story. Make of list of three or four of these. They can be anything you want, not just plot or world details. Next, if you had only *one* of those details to tell someone, which would it be?

   _____

   _____

   _____

   _____

   _____

3. Identify the twist in your novel. You have an interesting person with some interesting trait, something interesting about the world he or she lives in or the situation—now list what will surprise or shock readers. What's the unexpected detail that sets this story apart?

   _____

   _____

   _____

   _____

   _____

   _____

   _____

EXERCISE:
Identify the Key Elements for Your Summary Line

>>**Using all of your notes and previous exercises, answer the following questions:**

1. What is your idea? (page 21) _____

_____

_____

_____

_____

2. Is this a plot-driven or a character-driven novel? (page 20) _____

_____

_____

_____

3. Who is your protagonist? (page 27) _____

_____

_____

_____

4. Who or what is your antagonist? (page 32) _____

_____

_____

_____

5. What is the conflict type? (page 29) _____

_____

_____

_____

6. What are the core conflicts? (page 142) _____

_____

_____

_____

7. What is the protagonist's goal? (page 133) _____

_____

_____

_____

_____

8. What is the antagonist's goal? (page 139) _____

_____

_____

_____

_____

9. What are the stakes? (page 147) _____

_____

_____

_____

_____

10. What is the theme? (page 49) _____

_____

_____

_____

_____

11. What is the setting? (page 52) _____

_____

_____

_____

_____

12. What is the hook? (page 88) _____

_____

_____

_____

_____

ASSIGNMENT EIGHT:
Write Your Summary Line

By now you should have a pretty good idea what your novel is about, what the core conflict is, who your main characters are (both protagonist and antagonist), what their goals are, what the stakes are, the setting, the theme, and the hook. Some of the details might still be vague, but the foundation of the novel is there.

>>Put it all together and write your summary line.

If you're having trouble getting started, try this template:

[The protagonist] + [what's important about the story] + [the twist or hook].

Don't be afraid to mix it up or move the order around if that works better for your idea.

For example:

- ▶ Three teens with dark secrets meet at a roadside diner, unaware that one of them plans to reveal those secrets and destroy the others' reputations.
- ▶ A man in an unhappy marriage must find his inner hero during the zombie apocalypse to save the woman he truly loves.
- ▶ A workaholic entrepreneur and a risk-averse teacher from feuding families fall in love after the funeral of a beloved teacher draws them home and back into each other's lives.

_____

_____

_____

_____

_____

_____

Exercises for Workshop Nine:
Turning Your Summary Line
Into a Summary Blurb

These exercises will help you take the summary line and craft a summary blurb that captures the core plot elements of your novel. (Pages 201-230 in *PYN*)

Probably the most common summary blurb issue is not knowing how to condense your novel into a few sentences. This usually happens because you don't know what your story is about, and you've developed a premise novel. You see a lot of backstory and world building, but when you look close, you don't see a character actually trying to solve a problem. It reads more like set up than story. If you run into this, try figuring out what the protagonist is trying to accomplish. Find the core conflict of the novel and make sure that's what the protagonist is working toward solving the whole book.

The second most common issue is a lack of stakes. You'll see a lot of explanation about what happens, but little to no "why" or "why it matters." Or if there is a "why it matters," there are no consequences to the protagonist making that choice. Try to identify the risk the protagonist is taking and the consequence if she loses or fails. Let her choices have consequences and force her to make hard decisions. Nothing should be easy for her, and if she makes the wrong choice, very bad things should happen to her.

One of the roughest summary blurb problems is a novel that uses a well-loved idea, but doesn't put a fresh enough spin on it. You'll see common ideas, or generalities instead of something unique to your story. To freshen up a common idea, find new angles on your story. Remember, the same story can be told a million different ways. The plot that tells that story is where you want to be as original as possible. And plot is all about what happens to whom and why.

Sometimes we just have too much story for one book. We can't identify any one character driving the story and too many characters want our attention. To pare down, look for characters that can be merged into one, or weed out extra subplots that don't advance the core story.

The summary blurb is a great way to test your idea before you write it.

BRAINSTORMING QUESTIONS: Getting to the Heart of Your Story

Ask these three questions of your own idea. Use your notes to build the strongest and most compelling goal-motivation-stakes trio you can. (Page 203 of *PYN*)

1. What does the protagonist want?

_____

_____

_____

_____

Bonus Question. Why should a reader care about this want?

_____

_____

_____

2. Why does the protagonist want this?

_____

_____

_____

_____

Bonus Question. How will the reader relate to this?

_____

_____

_____

3. What about the protagonist's life will change if he or she fails?

_____

_____

_____

_____

Bonus Question. Will the reader worry about this? Why or why not?

_____

_____

_____

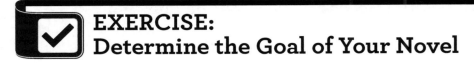

EXERCISE:
Determine the Goal of Your Novel

>>**Describe what your protagonist wants, why it matters, and how his or her life will change if he or she fails to get it.**

For example:

▶ Lana wants redemption and forgiveness for causing her brother's accident because the guilt is eating her alive, and if she doesn't get it she'll descend onto a dangerous path of trying to punish herself by acting recklessly.

▶ Bob wants to divorce Sally and be with Jane because he's miserable, and if he doesn't change his life he'll end up feeding Sally to the zombies just to get away from his misery.

▶ Adam wants to fill the empty void his life has become, because he fears he's turning into the despised person his business reputation says he is. If he doesn't change his ways, he'll be alone and unloved forever. Hannah wants some excitement and meaning in her life, because she's always played it safe and that hasn't brought her happiness. If she doesn't do something to shake up her life and seek out happiness, she'll wind up alone with a safe, predictable, but unhappy life.

_____

_____

_____

_____

_____

_____

_____

_____

_____

_____

_____

_____

_____

_____

_____

_____

💡 BRAINSTORMING QUESTIONS: Getting to the Heart of Your Conflict
Explore the potential hooks in your novel. (Page 210 of *PYN*)

1. What intellectual problem does your protagonist need to resolve?

_____

_____

_____

_____

_____

2. What are some story questions you want readers to wonder about?

_____

_____

_____

_____

_____

3. How are these questions going to be answered?

_____

_____

_____

_____

_____

4. What emotional problem is your protagonist facing?

_____

_____

_____

_____

_____

5. What emotions do you want readers to feel as they read your novel?

_____

_____

_____

_____

_____

EXERCISE:
Determine the Hooks of Your Novel

>>Describe the intellectual and emotional hooks.

The hooks can be phrased as questions readers might ask, or things you want to create in the story.

For example:

▶ **Intellectual Hook:** Who called the teens to the diner? What's the plan? Will their secrets be exposed?

Emotional Hook: Will Lana find redemption before she's exposed and loses her chance? Why does the bad guy want to hurt these people?

▶ **Intellectual Hook:** How did the zombie apocalypse happen? Is there a cure and will they find it?

Emotional Hook: Will Bob find the strength to tell Sally and Jane the truth, and if so, will it really make him happy?

▶ **Intellectual Hook:** What caused these two families to hate each other so much for so long?

Emotional Hook: Will Adam and Hannah be able to overcome their history, end the feud, and find love with each other?

_____

_____

_____

_____

_____

_____

_____

_____

_____

_____

_____

_____

_____

_____

_____

BRAINSTORMING QUESTIONS: Getting to the Heart of Your Setting
Think about where your novel is set and answer the following questions. (Page 215 of *PYN*)

1. What are the critical elements of the setting?

   _____

   _____

   _____

2. If you changed your setting, what else would change?

   _____

   _____

   _____

3. What type of inherent conflicts occur in this setting?

   _____

   _____

   _____

4. Is there a history that creates a deeper thematic meaning?

   _____

   _____

   _____

5. Does the setting allow you to make a point you couldn't otherwise make?

   _____

   _____

   _____

6. Does the setting provide a challenge for your characters you couldn't otherwise have?

   _____

   _____

   _____

Bonus Question. How common is this setting to your genre? Is it *too* common?

   _____

   _____

   _____

EXERCISE:
Embed the Setting Into Your Novel

>>Describe your setting as it pertains to your novel and the conflict of that novel.

For example:

▶ A roadside diner just outside of town, where few locals go but lots of traffic passes through. People are constantly coming and going, and any one of them could be the person who asked the trio there or could have something to do with why they're there.

▶ Cleveland during the zombie apocalypse, showing the world falling apart as Bob's life falls apart. The city is overrun, all of Bob's favorite places are destroyed or abandoned, his world is gone and just as lost as he feels.

▶ The small, southern town of Henderson, with quaint shops and streets, where everything *looks* perfect and wonderful. But in reality, it's all a lie, a facade used to hide the long-time family feud and decay of the town, suffering because the two sides can't make amends. Adam and Hannah are the key to fixing that and bringing new life and vitality back to the town (and the families).

>>Next, boil your setting down to one or two sentences (if your first description was longer).

For example:

▶ A rundown, roadside diner on the outskirts of town, perfect for a clandestine meeting

▶ Cleveland during the zombie apocalypse

▶ The small, southern town of Henderson, where everything looks perfect on the outside

_____

_____

_____

_____

_____

_____

_____

BRAINSTORMING QUESTIONS: The Inciting Event

Think about the moment in which your protagonist first discovers there's a problem, or the first step he or she takes that will become that problem. (Page 219 of *PYN*)

1. What is the event or moment that brings your protagonist into your core conflict?

_____

_____

_____

_____

_____

2. What's happening when the protagonist encounters or triggers that moment?

_____

_____

_____

_____

_____

3. How does this event connect to your core conflict?

_____

_____

_____

_____

_____

Bonus Question. Is there a catalyst problem in the opening that gets the protagonist to this event?

_____

_____

_____

Bonus Question. How much time passes between the opening page and the inciting event?

_____

_____

_____

EXERCISE:
Determine the Inciting Event of Your Novel

>>Describe your inciting event.

For example:

▶ Lana finds a note stuck in her locker at school, claiming someone knows what she did to her brother and that she'd better come to the diner tonight at nine o'clock or everyone will find out.

▶ Bob is working up the nerve to ask his wife for a divorce when he hears groaning and shuffling outside. He goes to check, thinking it's some kind of wild animal going through his trash. But it's a zombie, and it tries to eat him. He starts screaming and Sally rushes in and saves him, then totally takes charge of everything.

▶ Adam and Hannah are both notified that their favorite teacher has passed away, and each decides to attend her funeral despite being estranged from their families and not wanting to face home or their relatives again.

_____

_____

_____

_____

_____

_____

_____

_____

_____

_____

_____

_____

_____

_____

_____

_____

BRAINSTORMING QUESTIONS: Your Novel's Ending
Explore how your novel might end. (Page 222 of *PYN*)

1. What constitutes a win for your protagonist?

   _____

   _____

   _____

2. What constitutes a win for your readers?

   _____

   _____

   _____

3. How does your protagonist solve the core conflict problem of the novel?

   _____

   _____

   _____

4. How does this affect your protagonist?

   _____

   _____

   _____

5. What price does your protagonist pay for this resolution?

   _____

   _____

   _____

6. How do *you* want it to end?

   _____

   _____

   _____

Bonus Question. How does this ending resolve the problem triggered in the inciting event?

   _____

   _____

   _____

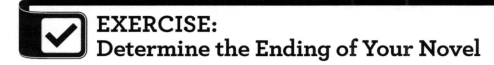

EXERCISE:
Determine the Ending of Your Novel

>>Describe the ending of your novel.

At this stage, you don't have to describe the ending in detail. Just try to figure out what the overall goal is, or what success means for the protagonist. If you're not sure, write down some options.

For example:

▶ Lana realizes saving Miguel from Zachary's plan will help her redeem herself for her role in her brother's accident—either by giving her the strength to confess or by making her realize she was never truly the cause.

▶ Bob finds his inner hero, proves he's a good man after all, and is finally able to ask Sally for a divorce and profess his love to Jane.

▶ Adam and Hannah fall in love, heal the wounded families, and live happily ever after.

_____

_____

_____

_____

_____

_____

_____

_____

_____

_____

_____

_____

_____

_____

_____

_____

_____

_____

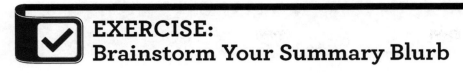

EXERCISE:
Brainstorm Your Summary Blurb

>>Answer the following questions about your novel:

- Who is the novel about?

_____

_____

_____

- What is the main problem to be faced?

_____

_____

_____

_____

- Where does the novel take place?

_____

_____

_____

- What triggers the novel's core problem?

_____

_____

_____

_____

- Why does it matter that this problem is resolved?

_____

_____

_____

- How does the novel end?

_____

_____

_____

ASSIGNMENT NINE:
Write Your Summary Blurb

>>**Put it all together and craft your summary blurb.**

A summary blurb can be basic information, or contain the voice or style of the novel. Sometimes it helps to use this exercise to get a feel for how a character might sound or what the novel's tone might be.

If you need a little help in crafting the blurb, try this general template. Feel free to move parts around as they pertain to your novel. This template is a guide to help you think, not something you have to follow exactly as written. You can even cut some of the parts out if they don't work.

[introduce the protagonist] is [tell a little about her] who [why she's in the right place to have something happen to her]. She [what leads her to the inciting event] where [the inciting event happens].

She [reacts to what's happened] and finds herself [how the inciting event has made a mess of the protagonist's life]. To [fix this problem] she must [the main thing that needs to be accomplished to win] before [the antagonist does what she needs to do]. If she doesn't, [why it's bad, and what she has to lose if she fails].

For example:

▶ [Lana] is [struggling to maintain her "everything is fine" facade at school after her brother is paralyzed in an accident]. She [receives a menacing note in her locker, threatening to expose her unless she agrees to meet at a roadside diner]. She goes, and [encounters two boys who also received similar notes].

She's [unsure who is behind this or how the other two boys are connected] and finds herself [fighting to uncover who is threatening them and why, before her secret is revealed to the entire town]. But to [uncover the person behind the threats] she must [reveal her secret to the two other boys] before [they're all exposed]. If she doesn't, [everyone will know she caused her brother's accident and she'll never get the forgiveness she craves].

_____

_____

_____

_____

_____

_____

_____

_____

_____

_____

Exercises for Workshop Ten:
Turning Your Summary Blurb
Into a Working Synopsis

These exercises will help you craft a working synopsis you can write a novel from. Remember, these are for you to organize your thoughts, so don't worry if the words are rough or don't make sense to anyone else. (Pages 232-301 in *PYN*)

While developing your working synopsis, think about how each of these moments will lead to the next and help your plot unfold. Pay special attention to words like *but, so,* and *therefore,* which usually indicate that a choice has been made or something has created change. The more of these you use, the more likely your plot is building off the individual scenes and character choices.

If you find a lot of *and then* connecting your scenes, that's a good indication that things are just "happening" without any real drive. You might even be able to reorganize the scenes and not change much about the story (another red flag). Ask yourself:

1. How many choices do I offer my protagonist?

Aim for scenes that give your protagonist a choice that could either raise the stakes or the tension, add unpredictability, or take the story in an unexpected direction.

2. How many obvious outcomes are there?

Try to avoid scenes that are solely about getting the protagonist from point A to point B. If the outcome is obvious and there's nothing to threaten the resolution, it lessens the mystery, tension, and even the stakes of the whole novel.

3. Where might you add more choices?

Choice creates mystery and unpredictability. Readers read to see what happens next, and the more uncertain the outcome, the more intrigued they'll be.

As you do these exercises, look for ways to connect these pieces to form a larger story. Develop the motivations and goals for your characters so they're driving the story, not just acting out a predetermined plot.

Tough choices lead to great stories.

BRAINSTORMING QUESTIONS: Defining Story Arcs
List the steps for potential arcs in your novel. (Page 244 of *PYN*)

1. **The plot arc:** Look carefully at what steps move the core plot from opening scene to resolution. Make a list of those steps, focusing on the moments that have to happen for the plot to work.

_____

_____

_____

_____

_____

_____

_____

_____

_____

_____

_____

_____

_____

_____

2. **The subplot arcs:** Consider potential subplots, especially any that connect strongly to the core conflict or character arc.

_____

_____

_____

_____

_____

_____

_____

_____

_____

_____

_____

3. **The character arcs:** Start with the protagonist and list all the events/revelations/failures that cause his character to grow or change. Next, look at the antagonist (if he plays an active role) and secondary characters.

_____

_____

_____

_____

_____

_____

_____

_____

_____

_____

_____

_____

_____

_____

_____

_____

_____

_____

_____

_____

_____

_____

_____

_____

_____

4. **The theme arcs:** Look for situations where the theme might appear, especially if it causes a change or influences a character. Make a list of all the areas where theme could be used.

    _____

    _____

    _____

    _____

    _____

    _____

    _____

    _____

    _____

    _____

5. **Timeline arcs:** List when major events happen to make sure there's enough time for things to occur, and things aren't happening out of order.

    _____

    _____

    _____

    _____

    _____

    _____

    _____

    _____

    _____

    _____

BRAINSTORMING QUESTIONS: The Opening Scene
Find your opening scene. (Page 251 of *PYN*)

1. What is a typical day like for your protagonist?

_____

_____

_____

_____

_____

_____

_____

2. What problems might occur in that typical day?

_____

_____

_____

_____

_____

3. What is the core conflict of your novel?

_____

_____

_____

_____

_____

4. What critical setting or world-building details are needed to understand the world?

_____

_____

_____

_____

_____

5. What is likable or compelling about your protagonist?

_____

_____

_____

_____

6. What is the first image you want readers to see?

_____

_____

_____

_____

_____

_____

_____

7. Is the opening scene the inciting event or a problem that leads to the inciting event?

_____

_____

_____

_____

_____

_____

_____

_____

8. How does the opening scene end?

_____

_____

_____

_____

_____

_____

_____

_____

_____

_____

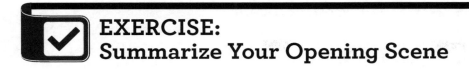

EXERCISE:
Summarize Your Opening Scene

>>Describe how your novel opens.

Be as detailed or as vague as you'd like. Try to end the scene with something that will create a goal that leads to the next scene.

It's not uncommon for this scene to change as you learn more about your novel and plot. As ideas hit you, come back and flesh out this summary.

If you're not sure how much to write, aim for one or two paragraphs that describe how the novel opens, what the protagonist is doing, why she's doing it, what goes wrong, what's at stake, and what the protagonist decides to do next. If you want to, continue summarizing how the plot would unfold to the next major turning point.

Feel free to add in any notes about what you want the scene to cover if you know conceptually what you want, but prefer to figure out the details during the writing process.

For example:

▶ Bob and Sally are arguing about what they plan to do that day. Sally has the day all scheduled doing things Bob doesn't want to do, and as much as he protests, she won't compromise. He says he has to work today and go into the office and she doesn't buy it. She starts belittling him as always, making him feel worthless. [Show how bad Bob's marriage is and why he wants to divorce his wife and get away.] (see *PYN page 257* for full example)

_____

_____

_____

_____

_____

_____

_____

_____

_____

_____

_____

_____

_____

💡 BRAINSTORMING QUESTIONS: The Inciting Event
Using the notes in Workshop Nine, further develop your inciting event. (Page 257 of *PYN*)

1. Write down the inciting event from Workshop Nine. (page 92) _____
   _____
   _____
   _____

2. How does the protagonist get to this moment from the opening scene? _____
   _____
   _____
   _____

3. What's the protagonist trying to do when this moment occurs? (the scene goal) _____
   _____
   _____
   _____

4. What is the conflict of the scene? _____
   _____
   _____
   _____

5. What's at stake in the scene? _____
   _____
   _____
   _____

6. How is this problem resolved? _____
   _____
   _____
   _____

7. Does this event also affect the protagonist's character arc? How? _____
   _____
   _____
   _____

8. How does the resolution trigger the next step of the plot? _____
   _____
   _____
   _____

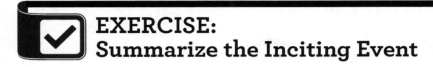

EXERCISE:
Summarize the Inciting Event

>>**Describe the moment where the protagonist's life changes and he starts on the path to the novel's core conflict.**

Be as detailed or as vague as you'd like. Consider how this scene builds off your opening scene and how it might lead to the next scene. Include any notes that might help later.

If you're not sure how much to write, aim for one to three paragraphs that describe how the protagonist went from the opening scene to the moment the inciting event happens, what he's trying to do, his reasons why, what goes wrong, what's at stake, and the decision that will transition to the next scene. Writing more is also acceptable if you want to continue with how the plot would unfold to the next major turning point.

For example:

▶ Bob has just about gathered enough courage to confront Sally about the divorce when he hears a weird moaning coming from outside. At first he ignores it, thinking it's an animal. But when the noises get louder and it sounds like things are getting knocked over, his built-up righteous anger sends him outside to investigate and give the trespasser a good lecture. (see *PYN page 260* for full example)

_____

_____

_____

_____

_____

_____

_____

_____

_____

_____

_____

_____

_____

_____

_____

_____

BRAINSTORMING QUESTIONS: The Act One Problem
Further develop your act one problem. (Page 262 of *PYN*)

1. What is the protagonist's goal and how does that lead to the core conflict?_____

_____

_____

_____

_____

2. What is motivating him to act?_____

_____

_____

_____

_____

3. What's at stake if he fails or refuses to act? _____

_____

_____

_____

_____

4. Where does this scene take place? _____

_____

_____

_____

5. Who else is in the scene? _____

_____

_____

_____

_____

6. Who else might be at risk? _____

_____

_____

_____

_____

7. How does this scene build off the inciting event?_____

_____

_____

_____

_____

8. What subplots might lead to this or cause additional trouble, both internal and external?

_____

_____

_____

_____

9. What choice does this problem present to the protagonist? _____

_____

_____

_____

_____

10. What conflicts affect this choice, both internally and externally? _____

_____

_____

_____

_____

11. How does this choice lead to the next goal? _____

_____

_____

_____

_____

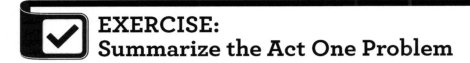

EXERCISE:
Summarize the Act One Problem

>>Describe the problem that ends with a choice, and how the protagonist got to that problem.

Be as detailed or as vague as you'd like. Consider how this scene builds off your beginning and how it might transition to the middle part of the novel. Include any helpful notes that come to you.

If you're not sure how much to write, aim for one to three paragraphs that describe what the problem is, how the protagonist ended up here, what choice he has to make, and how the stakes escalate. He had X problem, but now he has Y problem and has to decide what to do, which leads to the next scene. Writing more is also acceptable if you want to continue with how the plot would unfold to the next major turning point.

For example:

▶ Bob and Sally flee upstairs, zombies close behind them. They barricade themselves in the extra room and Sally breaks out the guns and camping gear (she keeps her adventure survival stuff in the spare room), and starts packing. She seems oddly prepared for this, though Bob doesn't really notice [lay groundwork for later reveal about her work at the lab]. He's still having a hard time coming to grips with what just happened, worrying about Jane and having no clue how to get to her. Sally snaps at him to suck it up and be useful, which angers him again. But he does what she orders and they figure out a quick plan to get out of the house and down to the fire station a few blocks away. They think they'll be safe there. It's on the way to the office, so he agrees, hoping the firemen can help with Jane's rescue. A small part of him wishes he could rescue her like Sally did him. Wouldn't he be the hero then? (see *PYN page 264* for full example)

_____

_____

_____

_____

_____

_____

_____

_____

_____

_____

_____

_____

BRAINSTORMING QUESTIONS: The Act Two Choice
Further develop your act two choice. (Page 272 of *PYN*)

1. What opportunity is offered at the end of act one?_____

_____

_____

_____

_____

2. Who is involved in this opportunity? _____

_____

_____

_____

_____

3. What are the choices offered?_____

_____

_____

_____

_____

4. How do these choices lead to the core conflict? _____

_____

_____

_____

_____

5. What are the consequences for making a choice? _____

_____

_____

_____

_____

6. How will this lead to the midpoint reversal? _____

_____

_____

_____

_____

_____

7. What possible subplots might result from these choices? _____

_____

_____

_____

_____

_____

8. What is the protagonist leaving behind in his "old world?" _____

_____

_____

_____

_____

_____

9. What new opportunities will the protagonist encounter going forward? _____

_____

_____

_____

_____

_____

Bonus Question. How might this choice illustrate the theme of the novel?

_____

_____

_____

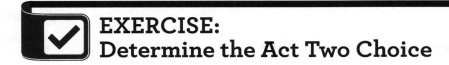

EXERCISE:
Determine the Act Two Choice

>>**Describe what your protagonist decides to do and how this sets him on the plot path to the midpoint.**

Be as detailed or as vague as you'd like. Consider how this scene might lead to the next turning point of the novel. Add notes as you see fit.

If you're not sure how much to write, aim for one to two paragraphs that describe what the choice is, why it's important, how it changes things for the protagonist, how the stakes escalate, and where the protagonist will go from here. Writing more is also acceptable if you want to continue with how the plot would unfold to the next major turning point.

For example:

▶ Bob decides to stay with Sally and figure out a way to convince her the office is the safest place and they need to go there (and save Jane in the process). He actually manages to get her to listen [find a clever way to show Bob does indeed have some skills] and they head off with several of the other survivors. [Is there a possible subplot to be had from one of the survivors? Maybe connected to Sally and the lab?] Bob is surprised Sally isn't leaving them behind, and wonders if she thinks they'll work as human shields. He feels guilty for thinking it since she did save most of them when she didn't have to. They make their way to the office building where Jane is. [Show various obstacles that illustrate Bob's weakness, him trying to step up and failing, Sally's disapproval, hints at her ulterior motive for agreeing to his plan—involves her job at the lab, maybe there's something in the same building she's after. Medical related?] Several close calls and a few deaths to show the stakes. (see *PYN page 274* for full example)

_____

_____

_____

_____

_____

_____

_____

_____

_____

_____

_____

BRAINSTORMING QUESTIONS: The Midpoint Reversal

Discover your midpoint reversal. (Page 276 of *PYN*)

1. What is the absolute worst thing that can happen to your protagonist at that moment?

_____

_____

_____

_____

_____

_____

2. How can you make that happen and force him to work overtime to get out of it?

_____

_____

_____

_____

_____

_____

_____

_____

3. Is there a way to make your protagonist's inner goal clash with his outer goal in a disastrous way?

_____

_____

_____

_____

_____

_____

4. What's the one thing that could happen that would make your protagonist give up?

_____

_____

_____

_____

_____

5. If this happened, what would keep him trying anyway?

_____

_____

_____

_____

_____

6. Are there any deep dark secrets that could be revealed and ruin everything?

_____

_____

_____

_____

_____

_____

7. How might the result _not_ be the one the protagonist was worried about—it's _worse_?

_____

_____

_____

_____

_____

8. Can you mirror the climax or foreshadow the ending or choice that is to be made later?

_____

_____

_____

_____

_____

Bonus Question. What's the last thing readers will expect to happen now? Can that happen?

_____

_____

_____

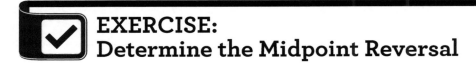

EXERCISE:
Determine the Midpoint Reversal

>>**Describe the midpoint reversal of your novel, and how it changes the life, goal, expectations, and/or beliefs of the protagonist.**

Be as detailed or as vague as you'd like. Consider how this scene might lead to the next turning point of the novel.

If you're not sure how much to write, aim for one to three paragraphs that describe how the protagonist reaches this moment, what happens, how it affects him, and where he has to go from here. Writing more is also acceptable if you want to continue with how the plot would unfold to the next major turning point.

For example:

▶ The gang makes their way to Jane's office and Bob is relieved to see her alive and well. She's also thrilled to see him, but not for the reason he'd have hoped. She's just glad to find someone else alive. Sally wants to know if she's heard any information about what's happening, and Jane updates them. She also shows them a radio/CB she stole from another office (who might have one of these? PI with a police scanner?) and says she's heard people calling for help and offering it, but those have been getting fewer and fewer. Bob is impressed with her resourcefulness and says so. Jane is pleased by the flattery. Sally is too distracted to notice. She pulls binoculars out of her survival bag and stares off into the distance toward her office building. She tries the radio and says some odd things, almost like a code. Bob has no clue what she's doing but figures it's something she learned from all her work retreats [set up that her office did survival retreats as team-building exercises]. When done, she pulls Bob aside and says they need to get to her building, but they can't bring the rest of these people. (see *PYN page 278* for full example)

_____

_____

_____

_____

_____

_____

_____

_____

_____

_____

BRAINSTORMING QUESTIONS: The Act Two Disaster
Discover your act two disaster. (Page 281 of *PYN*)

1. What is the thing that would make the protagonist want to give up?

_____

_____

_____

2. How might that happen in the story?

_____

_____

_____

3. How might the protagonist get to this point? What events need to happen before this occurs?

_____

_____

_____

4. What is the protagonist's flaw?

_____

_____

_____

5. How might this flaw cause the protagonist to fail, or lead the protagonist toward failure?

_____

_____

_____

6. What realization might the protagonist have that pulls him out of the dark night of the soul?

_____

_____

_____

7. How might the protagonist put this realization into practice? How might it change him?

_____

_____

_____

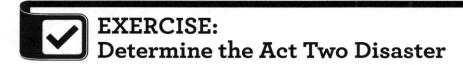

EXERCISE:
Determine the Act Two Disaster

>>**Describe what goes wrong or how the protagonist fails, and how this sets him up for the march to the novel's climax.**

Be as detailed or as vague as you'd like. Consider how this scene might lead to the climax of the novel.

If you're not sure how much to write, aim for one to three paragraphs that describe how the protagonist's flaw led him to this moment and what goes wrong, how this sends him to the all-is-lost moment—what he feels and how he reacts, what depths he sinks to during the dark night of the soul, and what realization comes to him that makes him pull himself up and devise a new plan. Writing more is also acceptable if you want to continue with how the plot would unfold to the next major turning point.

For example:

▶ Bob and Jane are both floored. How did she get vaccinated? Sally confesses that her lab has been working on a bio-weapon for years, and everyone on the project was vaccinated as a precaution. (Issues over her lying to him all these years about what she did.) Bob asks if she created the zombification virus. She says no, it was supposed to be something else, but it obviously had unforeseen side effects. There was a test on it a few days ago, and clearly something went very wrong. Jane wants to know if the vaccine will work for the survivors, and Sally says yes, as long as they haven't been exposed yet. After that, they'd need the cure, and there are only a few vials of that deep in the lab's vault. (see *PYN page 283* for full example)

_____

_____

_____

_____

_____

_____

_____

_____

_____

_____

_____

_____

_____

BRAINSTORMING QUESTIONS: The Act Three Plan
Discover your act three plan. (Page 290 of *PYN*)

1. What weaknesses might the protagonist have discovered about the antagonist that could be exploited?

   _____

   _____

   _____

2. What was the protagonist afraid to do before, but now has the courage to try?

   _____

   _____

   _____

3. How have the protagonist's old and new beliefs merged?

   _____

   _____

   _____

4. What insight has this new outlook given the protagonist?

   _____

   _____

   _____

5. What has to be done to reach the antagonist?

   _____

   _____

   _____

6. What skills might the protagonist use to defeat the antagonist?

   _____

   _____

   _____

Bonus Question. What unexpected twist might occur to upset the plan?

   _____

   _____

   _____

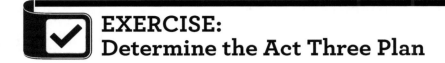

EXERCISE:
Determine the Act Three Plan

>>Describe what your protagonist plans to do to reach and defeat the antagonist.

Be as detailed or as vague as you'd like. Consider how this plan will lead to the climax of the novel.

If you're not sure how much to write, aim for one to two paragraphs that describe how the protagonist's dark night has given him new insights into what has to be done to win, how to go about reaching the antagonist, and what might be required to defeat her. Writing more is also acceptable if you want to continue with how the plot would unfold to the next major turning point.

For example:

▶ Sally finds a floor plan of the lab (fire escape route?) and sketches out a plan. She has no idea if the vault can even be opened, if there's any power to it, etc. (research vaults and security measures). The more she talks, the weaker she gets, and Bob realizes she was hurt a lot worse than he thought. He even hopes she's going to be okay. [Show how maybe they'll be okay after all and part as friends, maybe even work it out if they can't save Jane.] She gives him some of the gear (ammo, guns, etc.) and wishes him luck.

Bob sets off for the vault, encountering zombies and other obstacles along the way. [These will all be similar tests to what he failed in the first half of the book. Succeeding here shows how he's grown.] He gets to the vault, manages to bypass the security, and gets inside. He finds the cure, a single vial inside a case. He grabs it and heads back to Sally and Jane.

_____

_____

_____

_____

_____

_____

_____

_____

_____

_____

_____

_____

_____

BRAINSTORMING QUESTIONS: The Climax
Discover your novel's climax. (Page 293 of *PYN*)

1. What inner conflict has the protagonist been struggling with all along?

_____

_____

_____

2. How can the inner conflict butt heads with the outer problem in the climax?

_____

_____

_____

3. How might the inner conflict influence what the protagonist needs to do to solve the final problem?

_____

_____

_____

4. How might the theme be used to make the ending more powerful, and thus raise the stakes?

_____

_____

_____

5. How might the risk be more personal for the protagonist?

_____

_____

_____

6. What surprise might happen to throw either the protagonist or the antagonist off?

_____

_____

_____

7. How does the act three plan compare to the climax? Does it work as expected? Does it fail?

_____

_____

_____

EXERCISE:
Determine the Climax

>>Describe how the climax unfolds.

Be as detailed or as vague as you'd like. Consider how the climax resolves the core conflict of the novel.

If you're not sure how much to write, aim for one to three paragraphs that describe how the climax unfolds, where it takes place, what (if any) surprise occurs, and how the protagonist deals with that surprise to resolve the core conflict. Writing more is also acceptable if you want to continue with how the plot would unfold.

For example:

▶ When Bob returns to Sally, she's pale and in bad shape. He's concerned, but as he gets closer he notices something's not right. Sally asks if he got it. He doesn't want to tell her. She comes closer, aggressive though trying not to be. She demands he give it to her. She'll inject Jane with it. He says no. She says she's better suited to it, give her the vial. Bob is freaking out. Sally is changing, even though she was vaccinated. He says as much and she laughs. Says she guesses it wasn't as useful as they all hoped it would be, and no wonder the whole lab changed into zombies. She lunges for him and he barely avoids it. She's right on the verge of becoming a zombie, fast, strong, dangerous, and he doesn't know if he'll be able to beat her. He's not sure if he even should. Does she deserve the cure? Does he owe it to her? But he also thinks about how she was one of those responsible for this whole mess. He's still trying to decide when she goes full zombie. [Show how Sally has always been the antagonist, but here she becomes the symbol of everything bad that has happened.] (see *PYN page 296* for full example)

BRAINSTORMING QUESTIONS: The Wrap-Up
Discover your novel's wrap-up. (Page 298 of *PYN*)

1. What events might come after the climax?

_____

_____

_____

2. What final image might mirror the opening image?

_____

_____

_____

3. Where do you want your protagonist to be at the end of the novel?

_____

_____

_____

4. What mood or emotion do you want to leave readers with?

_____

_____

_____

5. What do you want readers thinking about after they've finished the book?

_____

_____

_____

6. If it's a series, what hints or questions do you want to dangle for the next book?

_____

_____

_____

Bonus Question. What questions (if any) do you want to leave unanswered?

_____

_____

_____

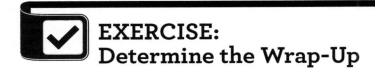

EXERCISE:
Determine the Wrap-Up

>>Describe how and where the protagonist ends the novel.

Be as detailed or as vague as you'd like. Consider what image you want to leave readers with at the end of your novel.

If you're not sure how much to write, aim for one to two paragraphs that show the change and where the protagonist is (physically and emotionally) at the end of the novel. Think about where he started out and how this final image works with that opening image.

For example:

▶ They make it out (at some point finding themselves in a kitchen so Bob can redeem himself where he failed in the opening scene) and manage to grab a truck. As they drive away, Jane is looking much better. They crash through obstacles and zombies and get to the open road. They're not sure where they're going, but at least they're together.

Jane refocuses and is more like herself. She thanks Bob for saving her. He says he loves her again, and she says she loves him, too. Bob grabs the radio and starts calling for other survivors. He wonders if one of them can create a cure from Jane's blood. Despite the world being in shambles around him, for the first time in a long time, Bob's happy and thinks there's hope for the future.

_____

_____

_____

_____

_____

_____

_____

_____

_____

_____

_____

_____

_____

_____

ASSIGNMENT TEN:
Write Your Working Synopsis

>>**Put it all together and write your working synopsis.**

If you need a little guidance, try using these reminder questions to guide you through:

1. How does the novel open?

_____
_____
_____
_____
_____
_____
_____

2. What is the first problem the protagonist faces?

_____
_____
_____
_____
_____
_____
_____

3. How does this problem lead to the inciting event?

_____
_____
_____
_____
_____
_____
_____

4. How does this lead to the core conflict and the larger act one problem?

_____

_____

_____

_____

_____

_____

5. How does this result in the protagonist facing a major choice?

_____

_____

_____

_____

_____

_____

6. How does this choice lead to a series of struggles and tests in the middle of the book?

_____

_____

_____

_____

_____

_____

7. What is the midpoint reversal?

_____

_____

_____

_____

_____

_____

_____

8. How does this lead to an increase of problems and attacks by the antagonist?

_____

_____

_____

_____

_____

_____

9. What is the act two disaster?

_____

_____

_____

_____

_____

_____

10. How does this disaster lead to the all is lost moment and the dark night of the soul?

_____

_____

_____

_____

_____

11. What results from that soul searching?

_____

_____

_____

_____

12. How does this create the new plan to act?

_____

_____

_____

_____

_____

_____

13. How does this plan lead to the final showdown with the antagonist?

_____

_____

_____

_____

_____

_____

14. How does that showdown unfold?

_____

_____

_____

_____

_____

_____

_____

15. What happens afterward?

_____

_____

_____

_____

_____

Time to Write!

Congratulations! You made it.

You've done a lot of work in this workbook, and now you should have a solid plan to write your novel. Since developing a novel is a complicated process, it's not uncommon to discover you still have a few holes to fill in. If so, return to the exercises you need to and strengthen the weak spots in your plan.

Another option is to go through the exercises one more time and see what's changed since your first pass. Odds are you came up with some great ideas while writing your summary blurb or working synopsis that can help you deepen the novel as a whole. Elements that were vague when you first brainstormed them have direction now, and you'll find layers and connections you originally didn't see.

If your goal is to dive in and start writing, then consider coming back after your first draft is done and doing some of the exercises again. They're excellent guides during the revision process as well.

I hope you've enjoyed the workshops and feel confident about writing (or revising) your novel. If you've found this book helpful, please share with friends or leave reviews on your favorite sites.

Most of all, best of luck and good writing!

Janice Hardy
May 2016

Glossary

Antagonist: The person or thing in the protagonist's path of success.

Backstory: The history and past of a character that affects his or her actions in a novel.

Conflict: Two sides in opposition, either externally or internally.

Core Conflict: The major problem or issue at the center of a novel.

Exposition: Narrative intended solely to convey information to the reader.

Filter Words: The specific words used to create narrative distance in the point-of-view character.

Freestylers: Writers who write out of chronological order and arrange the book afterward.

Genre: A category or novel type, such as mystery, fantasy, or romance.

Goal: What a character wants.

Hook: An element that grabs readers and makes them want to read on.

Inciting Event: The moment that triggers the core conflict of the novel and draws the protagonist into the plot.

Logline: A one-sentence description of the novel.

Market: The demographic traits of the target audience for the novel, such as adult or young adult.

Narrative Distance: The distance between the reader and the point-of-view character.

Narrative Drive: The sense that the plot is moving forward.

Outline: The structured overview of how a novel will unfold, typically written as a guide before the novel is written.

Outliners: Writers who write with a predetermined outline or guide. They know how the book will end and how the plot will unfold before they start writing it.

Pacing: The speed of the novel, or how quickly the story moves.

Pantsers: Writers who write "by the seat of their pants," without outlines. They often don't know how the book will end or what will happen before they start writing it.

Plot: The series of scenes that illustrate a novel. What happens in the novel.

Point of View: The perspective used to tell the story.

Premise: The general description of the story.

Protagonist: The character driving the novel.

Query Letter: A one-page letter used to describe a novel when submitting a manuscript to an agent or editor.

Scene: An individual moment in a novel that dramatizes a goal or situation.

Series: Multiple books using the same characters and/or world.

Set Pieces: The key moments or events in a novel.

Setting: Where the novel takes place.

Sequel (1): A second book that continues where the first book leaves off.

Sequel (2): The period after a scene goal is resolved where the character reflects on events and makes a decision to act.

Single-Title Novel: A romance novel that isn't part of a publisher's category.

Stakes: What consequence will befall the protagonist if she fails to get her goal.

Stand-Alone Novel: A novel that contains one complete story in one book.

Structure: The framework a novel is written in, typically based on established turning points at specific moments in the novel.

Tension: The sense of something about to happen that keeps readers reading.

Theme: A recurring idea or concept explored in the novel.

Trilogy: A story that is told over the course of three books.

Trope: An idea or literary device commonly employed in a particular novel type.

Word Count: The number of words contained in a novel.

Thanks!

Thank you for using the *Planning Your Novel Workbook*. I hope you found it useful!

- Reviews help other readers find books. I appreciate all reviews, whether positive or negative. Please let others know what you thought about this book.

- Would you like more writing tips and advice? Visit my writing site, Fiction University at Fiction-University.com, or follow me on Twitter at @Janice_Hardy.

- Check out the other books from Fiction University: *Planning Your Novel: Ideas and Structure, Revising Your Novel: First Draft to Finished Draft,* and *Understanding Show, Don't Tell (And* Really *Getting It)*. Visit Fiction University for future writing guides in both my Foundation of Fiction and my Skill Builders series.

- I also write fantasy adventures for teens and 'tweens. My novels include The Healing Wars trilogy: *The Shifter, Blue Fire* and *Darkfall* from Balzer+Bray/HarperCollins, available in paperback, e-book, and audio book formats.

About the Author

Janice Hardy is the founder of Fiction University, a site dedicated to helping writers improve their craft. Her popular Foundations of Fiction series includes *Planning Your Novel: Ideas and Structure*, a self-guided workshop for planning or revising a novel, the companion *Planning Your Novel Workbook*, and *Revising Your Novel: First Draft to Finished Draft*. Her Skill Builders series begins with *Understanding Show Don't Tell (And* Really *Getting It)*.

She's also the award-winning author of the teen fantasy trilogy *The Healing Wars,* including *The Shifter, Blue Fire,* and *Darkfall,* from Balzer+Bray/Harper Collins. *The Shifter* was chosen for the 2014 list of "Ten Books All Young Georgians Should Read" from the Georgia Center for the Book. It was also shortlisted for the Waterstones Children's Book Prize (2011), and The Truman Award (2011).

She lives in Central Florida with her husband, one yard zombie, two cats, and a very nervous freshwater eel.

Visit her online at her author's site at www.janicehardy.com or learn about writing at www.fiction-university.com.

She also tweets writing links from @Janice_Hardy.

Made in the USA
San Bernardino, CA
15 August 2016